Still Goin'

This book is dedicated to;
Kate and Irene
(the two luckiest girls in the world)
and
Erika, Wendy and the staff at
Waterstones, EK

Still Goin'

Craig Stevenson and John Mackay

Cheapwayround Publishers
East Kilbride

Copyright @ 2012 Craig Stevenson and John Mackay

First published in 2012 by
Cheapwayround Publishers

ISBN No; 978 0 9570252 1 9

Typeset in East Kilbride by
Cheapwayround Publishers

Printed and Bound by
Bell and Bain Ltd.,
Burnfield Road, Thornliebank,
Glasgow, G46 7UQ

Cheapwayround Publishers
22 Balfour Terrace
East Kilbride, G75 0JQ

cheapwayround@hotmail.co.uk
www.cheapwayroundpub.co.uk

CONTENTS;

	Introduction	7
1.	Blown Away in Irvine	10
2.	Steamin' Doon the Clyde	32
3.	Blitzed in Clydebank	50
4.	We wiz Framed	68
5.	Bordering on a Dry Run	86
6.	Rothesay, it's a Wee Bute	108
7.	Away for a Wee Paddle	126
8.	Stoned in the Granite City	144
9.	Glasgow, Goin Roon an Roon	162
10.	The Pub That Time Forgot	184
11.	Dundee-a Piece o' Cake	203
12.	Lanarkshire; Scotland's Middle Earth?	221
13.	A Capital Day Oot	239

Introduction

Travelling around the country, usually by bus, is what we do by way of a hobby. Nobody forces us to do it. We volunteered. It suits us both as we get to combine three of our favourite pastimes; sightseeing, beer sampling and of course arguing about the quality of the first two of those pastimes.

Between us we have many years of experience in both of these subjects, with a special emphasis on the beer swilling. So it was no real stretch for us to start writing about our little adventures. At first it was meant to be just a bit of fun for us, but it soon got out of hand. Before we knew it we were talking about producing a book. Although it turned out to be a lot more complicated than we first thought it would be, we did manage to come up with a fairly accurate record of our day trips.

After the success of that first book, 'The Cheap Way Round', it became obvious, to us at least, that it was our duty to continue checking out the drinking dens of Scotland. This time around we thought it might be a good idea to produce a more in depth study of the bar trade.

Over the course of our extensive travels we have come across some pretty grotty drinking establishments. Our problem was that, unfortunately but possibly not too surprisingly, in many cases we did tend to fit right in with them. The thing is, it's not just the fixtures and fittings which make or break a good bar.

We don't always agree about the important matters of life, in fact alarm bells usually start ringing when we do concur. It's either a sign that we've been over indulging a little or, for some other reason, we haven't been paying attention. On the subject of bar staff however we are in complete accord. We've always believed that even the worst dive of a place could be saved by employing a competent barman. It's all in the service.

It is easy enough to prattle on about bogging toilets and bar rooms which haven't seen a paint brush in thirty years but grading staff is another thing entirely. We have been lucky enough to meet some really good barmen/women on our travels and, of course there have been quite a few we've met out there who shouldn't be allowed to stand in front of a bar never mind behind one.

In order to highlight the good from the bad and the ugly, we needed a benchmark, something to compare the different levels of service we encounter 'out in the field'.

Our favourite barman, as he likes to refer to himself, Russell, came to the rescue. As Scotland's self-proclaimed, greatest barman, he suggested that we use him as our benchmark. Being too lazy to look any further and of course not wanting to huff him, it's never a good idea to annoy the bar staff, we both agreed right there and then to adopt the **Russell Standard**.

It is quite certain that he will be a lot less than chuffed if we find too many bar staff out there who manage to reach his lofty standards.

We decided that, given our liking for the produce of the brewer's trade, it would be apt to use the image of a full beer glass as the single units in our scale.

The top of that scale is- 🍺🍺🍺🍺🍺, which is on a par with Russell's best efforts.

Below that-🍺🍺🍺🍺, 🍺🍺🍺, 🍺🍺, and 🍺 indicate a gradual decline in acceptable standards of service.

Three and above would be quite acceptable-below that we are talking about people best avoided. It was only after we started out on our travels once again that we discovered, to our horror, that it was possible to score even less than one Russell🍺. And so, it was with great sorrow that we had to introduce an image, which often brings a tear to even the most hardened drinkers eye, the empty beer glass-🍺.

Gaining this score really takes some doing. If there is any justice, being awarded it will prove to be the kiss of death for any pub that gets it.

Actually we are not that hard to please when it comes to service in public houses. Quite obviously, the length of time it takes to get served is vitally important. Far too often we have been left waving our arms around like windmills trying to get noticed by a reluctant barman or woman.

In many pubs, particularly the trendier ones, the older you are the longer you're going to have to hang around looking ridiculous before they kindly allow you to spend your hard earned cash.

Being quick off the mark to serve the more mature customer will always gain high marks from us.

A bit of patter also goes a long way towards gaining our praise. It doesn't have to be particularly funny or even topical. In fact we don't mind if it's completely insincere nonsense. Just a friendly word, that's all we ask.

The beer itself is also very important. It has to be good, and if it's also cheap, then so much the better. Although the staff can't really be expected to do much about the price of the hootch they are selling, we believe that since they are on the front line they can expect to catch some of the flack.

Presentation is something they can do something about though. Sliding a headless pint along the bar, in a glass which is borderline septic, is just not on.

Just for a bit of fun we thought it would be interesting to grade each journey using the points scored that day. This would give us a league table of all the trips we have done.

It threw up some interesting figures. However we are not entirely sure they can be seen as an accurate picture of the state of Scotland's bar trade, since we did visit some very odd pubs, run by some equally odd bar staff which tended to bring down the average scores with a resounding thump.

What should be remembered of course is that all the opinions expressed in the following chapters are just that: opinions. For the most part we see the pubs we review at the worst possible time of day. Because of the way we travel, it is usually either mid-morning to early evening when we check the places out. If that wasn't bad enough, we are always in a hurry. Buses, as we have found to our cost, wait for no man, so we have little choice. What we do have is a lot of fun.

Obviously trailing around the nation's pubs is not for everyone. But just getting out and about is always worthwhile. Meeting friends, old and new, helps to keep both body and mind active. So if you are lucky enough to have a bus pass, get out there and use it.

Blown Away in Irvine

**(First trip for the bus pass pair
Slightly marred by the Irvine air.)**

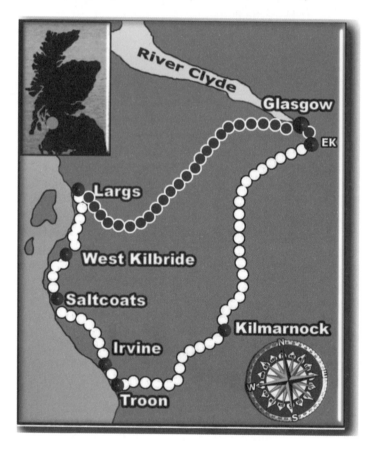

*East Kilbride-Troon-Irvine-Saltcoats-
West Kilbride-Largs-Glasgow*

John; This was the first trip of our second book, assuming we do a second book. This time we decided to try and cover more of Scotland, and why not, it's all free. We had also heard of a magical Gold Bus which is not only free, but that you get tea and scones for nothing as well.

We decided that we must try it sometime in a future trip, but back to our first trip.

As I was making up my usual pieces of corned beef with English mustard on plain bread (how I've missed them since our last trip a few months ago) Kate said that she had received an e-mail from Irene (Craig's wife) saying that she was going to have to look after her grandson that day and Craig had agreed that they could come on the trip with us. I was astonished. I could imagine me possibly being talked into Kate coming with us, but no way would Craig allow this to happen. I was really surprised and depressed at the idea when Kate put me out of my misery by shouting, April Fool!! What a woman, and a lucky one too. Lucky for her I didn't put her over my knee, although she did ask.

After getting over the shock, I ate my breakfast and at 9.20am, headed down to Craig's house to start our historic first journey of our second book.

Irene gave us a run to the EK bus station as it was pouring and blowing a gale. We got on the 9.46am X16. Craig, who had planned this trip with military precision, was confident of a trouble free trip. Amazing faith for a man who struggles with what time of day it is.

Craig: *After a break of three or four months, we decided it was time to get back on the buses. We missed the open road, we missed Scotland's scenic grandeur and of course we missed having a ready-made excuse to hang about pubs in the middle of the day.*

This time around we decided to approach our travels in a more professional manner. At one of our intensive brain storming

11

sessions, held as ever in "The Lum", it was agreed that we should broaden our horizons and see a bit more of the country, not to mention a more varied selection of its public houses. As John pointed out at the meeting there were far too many great wee country pubs out there which haven't been visited by us yet. It was time to put that right.

To travel the length, and quite possibly the breadth, of the country, we plan to make use of the new long distance coach routes which have recently been introduced. The shorter trips will follow the usual pattern.

The first journey in our latest odyssey took place on the 1st of April, 2011. Alarm bells should have been ringing as soon as I looked at the calendar. I would like to say the date didn't bother me since I'm not superstitious. The truth however is more frightening. I forgot to check the date before I started planning this trip. Not a good omen really.

Since it was still getting dark relatively early, we decided to keep things quite local. Our destinations for the day were Troon, Irvine, Saltcoats, West Kilbride and Largs.

At some time or other I have been to four out of the five of these towns and have mixed feelings about them.

The weather forecast for the day was surprisingly accurate, for once, so the umbrellas we carted around with us all day remained perfectly dry.

As seasoned travellers, we carry only essential items, sandwiches, the odd chocolate biscuit and on occasion, a piece of fruit. I once made the mistake of offering John a small packet of raisins Irene had packed for me. Word somehow got back to John's wife, Kate, and now we are both lumbered with more dried fruit than any man should ever be asked to consume. Things could quite easily get out of hand and we could end up in serious danger of eating healthily.

When we first started busing around Scotland I used a small rucksack to hold all this stuff. Very soon I realised that there were drawbacks to using luggage on our unique style of travelling. After a certain amount of travel and refreshments, the bag would start to misbehave. It would hide under tables, tie itself round my ankles or swing around hitting fixtures, fittings and innocent bystanders. The solution was to make everything disposable. That is to say swap the rucksack for a plastic poke.

This worked well for a while. Actually it worked up until this latest trip. While scurrying through the town centre in East Kilbride I caught a glimpse of our reflections in a large shop window. It was a depressing sight. Both of us had turned up with bright orange Sainsbury's bags. We looked like a couple of old dossers in search of a cosy shop doorway to sleep in. It could have been worse I suppose, we could have both been pushing supermarket trolleys. Anyway, it wasn't a good look.

John; Our first port of call on this historic day was Troon, so Craig had planned to get the X16 to Prestwick Airport, then cross the road and get the No. 14, I think, to Troon. I felt this was a bit hopeful as there was only three minutes between getting off the X16 and catching the No. 14 to Troon. There was a big dual carriageway we had to cross which involved going up and over a walkway, and Craig in particular is no Usane Bolt.

I told Craig of my feelings about the closeness of the transfer in a mocking sort of way so he had no option but to say he was right and it would be ok. I was hoping we would miss the No. 14 bus so I could start our trip by slagging off Craig. That's what friends are for.

As we approached the bus station in Kilmarnock I had the great idea of changing buses so we could get a local one to Troon. I felt this would give Craig an excuse to change the route and avoid the embarrassment of missing the next bus.

As we drove into the bus station, we could not see where the other buses were going as they were parked front in.

Amazingly (I am easily amazed) when we parked, a bus marked for Troon came in beside us. I made the dynamic decision to change buses (they're all free). The bus we left was not very comfortable and all steamed up, so we were glad to get off, especially Craig who by now was sweating over missing the No. 14 bus, but he didn't admit it.

Craig: The trip down to Kilmarnock was completely uneventful. Due to weather conditions the legendary scenic grandeur of Ayrshire was hidden from sight. The windows were so steamed up we might as well have been sitting inside a freight container.

Good beer and good cheer, just don't forget your credit card.

I had spent a lot of time putting the itinerary for this trip together. It was a masterpiece of planning. As far as I was concerned the hours I'd put in on the computer had paid off, giving us a perfectly workable schedule. There was just one potential problem which could scupper all my careful work. The thing was if our first bus was even just a few minutes late we would be sunk.

John started panicking about our first bus connection almost as soon as we left East Kilbride. By the time we reached Kilmarnock his paranoia had worn me down. I tried to put a brave face on things, as ever, telling him everything would work out just fine, but eventually I agreed to switch buses. Secretly I was quite glad. There was every chance that it would take me more than the five minutes I had allowed for the transfer between buses just to get out of my seat and up to the door. My back was playing me up again.

John: The Troon bus was much nicer and took us through a few local small villages before going into the outskirts of Troon. I was all chuffed as my decision meant a nicer bus, more interesting places passed, but more importantly, we should be in Troon earlier to allow us to be ready for opening time at 11.00am.

As usual, my joy was short lived, as the bus decided to detour through every road in the outskirts of Troon. Craig was smirking as the bus we should have got on passed us on its way out of Troon. However, I thought it was still a better journey and knew Craig agreed internally. We would have missed the thing anyway and ended up standing in the rain at Prestwick Airport.

We got off in Troon town centre at about 11.00am (opening time). Craig had told me he lived in Troon for a year many years ago. I think Craig's been chased out of a few towns in his time.

The rain was off so we had a wander about and headed along a street toward the marina area and went into *"The Anchorage"*. As usual, we were the first in. It was very nice, but not in the way we like. It was not an old man's pub. It was clean and our two pints cost about £6.60! What's that all about? We spoke to the barman, who was also the owner. He told us that business was quite good, but he made most of his money from the food. We had a look at the menu on the wall and could see he would make a fortune from the food if anyone was daft enough to buy it. The food costs were just as ridiculous as the pints. We reckoned they must get a lot of the Marina types who can afford to be ripped off. So although the prices were a bit of a rip off, the barman was friendly and helpful and the pub, although modern, was comfy.

We finished our pints in a pleasant atmosphere and the man even gave Craig a replacement poly bag for nothing. His was falling apart. I was happy he had changed for we both had Sainsbury poly bags. People must have been thinking we were living together.

Barman Rating; 🍺🍺🍺 (prices were high but barman was ok) Leaving *"The Anchorage"*, and a big hole in the kitty behind, we wandered back along the street away from Marina land and I had a couple of my pieces as we walked-they were brilliant.

The rain was off and it was pleasant as we wandered back up the main street and into what looked more like a man's pub. It was called *"The Lonsdale"* and fitted our requirements better-two pints were a fiver. Imagine being pleased at two pints costing a fiver. A couple of years you would have paid about half that-bloody ridiculous if you ask me-which you're not.

It was a typical old man's pub, with about half a dozen blokes who were obviously regulars and out of work, or too lazy to be bothered. We fitted in well.

The barman and the locals obviously knew we were tourists and ignored us although they were not threatening. We felt the barman at least could have asked us who we were and what we were doing in his pub. A bit of aggression is better than being ignored. **Barman rating;** 🍺

As we had nearly two hours in Troon, we still had time for further exploring, so we wandered up the street and into a pub called McKays. Not the Scottish way to spell my name (which is Mackay) but thought I'd mention it in the hope of educating you.

The pints were ok, not as cheap as *"The Lonsdale"*, but cheaper than *"The Anchorage"*. The people behind the bar were very quiet, so there was not much atmosphere in the place. You would think people would want to talk to you and make you feel welcome.

I don't think many barmen in Scotland realize that they are the most important thing in the bar, or maybe they don't care. The usual Scottish hospitality.

Barman Rating;

"The Lonsdale" got our vote as the best of the three pubs, and the cheapest, which helped. This was starting to look like a 10+ pinter day.

So after two or three visits to the toilets, we wandered out and our next bus, the No. 14 to Irvine, turned up on time. An uneventful 20 minute journey got us to Irvine.

Craig: Our new local bus took us on a little tour of Kilmarnock which suited me just fine. I went to school in the town and got my first job there as well. So it was a bit of a trip down memory lane for me.

John on the other hand was getting a bit worried that we might not get to Troon for a long, long time. Just when he thought we had made it to our stop the bus turned away from the town centre and into another labyrinth of back streets.

We had travelled for about ten or fifteen minutes before anyone got off the bus. Then to John's annoyance the dammed bus retraced its route back to the main road. I'm quite sure John would have happily sprung for a taxi for the old biddy who got off if he'd known how long it would take to get her to her house.

Blown Away in Irvine

The year I spent in Troon some years ago stood me in good stead for the mystery tour our driver took us on.

Troon is generally reckoned to be a bit up-market and there does seem to be a large number of retired, well heeled, people living in Troon.

I enjoyed the time I had spent there although it was a little on the quiet side for me.

In its heyday Troon was a very busy resort town. I once saw a selection of old postcards which were being displayed in a shop window. They were from the late 50s and 60s and showed large crowds of people on the beaches of Troon and Brassie. Nowadays very few of the locals ever bother visiting the beach. Then again I suppose Zimmers can be hard to handle in all that loose sand.

Back when I stayed in the town there were two main differences between me and the vast majority of Troon's population. I had no grey hair and no money. Unfortunately only one of those situations has changed in the intervening years. I'll let you guess which one. The one good thing to come of all our touring around the housing estates of Troon was that by the time we got off the bus the pubs were open. Before we entered our first pub of the day, I thought it would be a good idea to give John the grand tour. Unfortunately it had been 15 years since I lived there so it wasn't much of a tour. It mostly consisted of me saying "that wasn't there back then" or "that used to be something else". After my short lecture on urban redevelopment we made a bee line for "The Anchorage".

As soon as we opened the door it was evident that this was a bit upmarket for us. The carpet didn't stick to the soles of our shoes which is always an indication of class in my book. Actually it was a very well laid out pub. Very bright and clean, pity about the beer though. I think the proprietor was on a one man crusade to balance the national debt.

I would recommend this pub, but only to very rich or teetotal friends. After our pint we decided it was time to get some sawdust under our feet instead of shag pile.

"The Lonsdale" fitted the bill perfectly. I could be exaggerating of course as sawdust might be viewed as an unnecessary luxury by the patrons of this pub. It was a bit grim. We didn't exactly make a grand entrance. In fact we almost ended up behind the bar. Anywhere else the customers would have laughed at our stupidity when we eventually made it into the actual bar area. Not here. Perhaps laughing is banned in this place. Enjoyment certainly seems to be at a premium.

On the bright side the beer was cheap. But that was not enough to keep us there. Just before deep depression set in we set off to find another pub.

A home from home for Mr. Mackay perhaps?

Blown Away in Irvine

When we spotted "McKay's" (John's name spelt wrongly), we just had to go in. It was a step up from "The Lonsdale". The down side of our move to new, brighter surroundings was a fairly hefty increase in the price of the booze. The clientele was more mixed than 'The Lonsdale'. There were even some women in the place.

We didn't have much time to spend in this bar so we drank our beer at a fair old pace. Fortunately the bus stop was just outside and we made it there just in time for our next bus.

John; I know Irvine quite well as Kate's sister Sheila (who now lives in Rothesay) and their mum and dad lived there for many years. I decided to take Craig into a pub just off the main cross in Irvine called "*The Delta*". I knew from a visit there many years ago that it was a bit of a dump, and as we both like this type of pub, Craig said he would give it a go. He was not let down. This place gave word dump a bad name-it was a disaster.

As we went in people were running about trying to escape to the toilets and out windows, or would have if there had been any. Some bloke had farted-the place was disgusting-but the culprit seemed quite pleased with himself. I have a mate Big John who's a bit like that.

We hovered about outside till the cloud cleared and, god knows why, went in. The smell of shit was the best thing about the place. Hard to believe, but in we went and when we ordered our drinks, the barmaid apologised for the smell in the place, which was good of her, and we did enjoy our pints, which were cheap (about a fiver). The place was full of jakies, of all ages. This country is going to the dogs. Before we left, I went to the toilet (it was like a breath of fresh air) and the farter was in having a slash as well. He started to talk to me as if nothing had happened, talking about the weather and normal things. On his way out I noticed he had skid marks on the outside of his white tracky trousers.

Although the place smelled were fairly disgusting, the barmaid was pleasant and the pints tasted better than they smelt.

Protesters gather to demonstrate outside Irvine's toxic weapons testing facility.

Barmaid Rating; ♜♜♜ (can't be easy working in that atmosphere)

We were so put off Irvine by this episode, that we decided to get an earlier bus to our next stop, Saltcoats!

Craig: Irvine is only a few minutes along the road, but it has a totally different atmosphere to that of Troon. It's supposed to be an industrial town but nowadays there is not much industry around. That leaves a lot of spare time to hang around bars through the day.

John's choice of bar was not exactly inspired, unless of course he was trying to inspire fear and loathing. The "Delta Bar" was a dive. It was a smelly dive. Some of its patrons reeked a bit as well.

I'm not a great fan of pub entertainment at the best of times. But the floor show in the Delta was off the scale. The pub comedian seemed to think it was hilariously funny to loudly pass wind. After letting rip he would look around the place as if expecting wild applause. I suppose you could say he did bring a tear to my eye, but I assure you it wasn't brought on by laughter.

We couldn't get a seat in the place which was probably just as well. One pint was enough; after all, you can only hold your breath for so long.

Out on the street we spied a bus heading for Saltcoats and decided to jump aboard. That sounds a lot more dynamic than it really was. Shuffled would be a more accurate description of our exit from Irvine.

John; The run to Saltcoats takes you through Kilwinning, where Kate's other sister Margaret lives. Kilwinning's claim to fame is that Scotland's first Masonic Lodge, Lodge No. One is situated in the main street, just opposite a great wee baker's who do brilliant onion pies.

By the way, did you know that the way to tell an onion pie on the shelf as opposed to a normal pie is that the onion pie has two holes in the crust and the normal pie has only one. When I was told this I thought it was just a local Kilwinning two hole custom, but I have since found out that the two hole onion pie is international. That means the same all over the West of Scotland.

Going back to The Masonic Lodge information, it is simple. Kilwinning is a prodie town. This means, for the non-West of Scotland readers, that the majority of the population are prodies. (Ayrshire's equivalent of Lanarkshire's Larkhall).

An easy way to tell what the religious leanings of a particular town is that the prodie ones have Union Jacks hanging outside some of the pubs, normally in the rougher areas.

Leaving Kilwinning behind, the bus went through Stevenson, all I know about Stevenson is that it has a nice wee nine hole golf course which I played now and again with Robert, Kate's sister Margaret's late husband, a nice guy and a great golfer. Leaving Stevenson behind, the bus took us straight into Saltcoats. We got off (our first mistake) and had a walk along the main street, which is one of these pedestrian streets with most of the shops shut and very depressing. My Granny told me once that if you have nothing nice to say about someone (or I suppose someplace) then say nothing. So I have nothing to say about Saltcoats. This may be a bit unfair on Saltcoats as I'm sure it will be nice down at the beach and other areas we didn't visit. I feel I must say this in case we ever return.

We had a pint in a pub called "Swaney Beans" which after our experience in Irvine, seemed a nice wee pub (compared to 'The Delta Bar'). Mind you, the people in the place looked as hard as nails, and I was only looking at the women.

Craig said the name of the pub had a great history behind it, he may mention it in his version of today's trip. I was not listening to him as my mind was in terror in case I looked at someone the wrong way.

We finished our pints and got the hell out of the place as quickly as possible without looking as if we were getting out of the place as quickly as possible.

That fact that the barman had ignored us was a bonus in this pub.

Barman Rating; 🍺🍺🍺 (terrified to give him less in case he reads this, if he can read)

We arrived back at the bus stop and after checking the times realised that we would have time for another pint, so we found "Bobby's Bar" which compared to the last two pubs we were in was quite nice, although drink is definitely more expensive in pubs where nobody is allowed to fart or scare the shit out of you. My main complaint again is that the barman ignored us.

Barman Rating;  (wasn't as scared of this bloke)

Nice place to visit, but don't eat the pies.

While we waited for our next bus (the 585) to get us the hell out of Saltcoats, Craig texted Irene to tell here we were a bit ahead of schedule and were heading for *"The Tavern"*. This bar is in Millport, and it is conceivable that we could have got over to Millport for a quick pint. Millport is Irene's favourite place in the world and Craig knew she would be fuming. We were in fact heading for *"The Tavern"* in West Kilbride. Of course Irene didn't know this and two minutes later Craig's mobile rang. It was Irene going off her head. What a laugh, a good April Fool for Craig on Irene. Although I think tricks are supposed to be done before noon-who cares-it was funny.

Craig: Leaving Irvine behind seemed like a good idea. Anywhere would be an improvement after all. That's the kind of clever thinking that always gets us into trouble.

Although it was on our route we had decided to miss out on a refreshment stop in Kilwinning. We didn't have enough time to spare and of course we were too feart.

Many years ago I was unlucky enough to be in a car crash on the outskirts of the town. I was a passenger in the car which was badly damaged. We pushed it up on to the grass verge just as the police arrived. The sergeant told us we would be wise not to leave it there overnight. As he put it "That's Kilwinning down there pal. There'll be nothing left of your motor by tomorrow morning".

Kilwinning has a bit of a reputation for being on the rough side.

I have passed through Saltcoats many times before, usually when on a train journey between Glasgow and Ardrossan on my way to Arran. This coloured my opinion of Saltcoats, it has to be said. Railways tend to run through the less affluent parts of town. The embankments are usually strewn with litter, old mattresses and derelict buildings.

All of this can make even the nicest town look pretty bad. That's my theory anyway. There are, however, exceptions to every theory, and Saltcoats is definitely an exception. The main street is anyway. In fact, running a railway line up the middle of it would be an improvement.

The first pub we decided to visit was called "Sawney Beans". The name should have served as a warning, but it didn't. We were in need of beer.

It did however give me a chance to bore John rigid with a little bit of Ayrshire history. Sawney Bean was an infamous Ayrshire cannibal who travelled around apparently enjoying, in the most literal sense of the phrase, having people for dinner.

Legend has it that Sawney Bean was the head of an incestuous and cannibalistic family who robbed and murdered travellers who ventured along coastal routes near Ballantrae.

These unlucky travellers would be butchered, pickled and salted to see the family through the winter months. All of this supposedly took place in the 15th century

What possessed anyone to name their pub after him I'll never know. That being said, old Sawney did live in a dark cave so maybe there are comparisons to be drawn.

We didn't actually see any menu for bar meals, but rest assured we had made up our minds that under no circumstances whatsoever would we be trying out any of their meat pies.

We were less than impressed with some of the patrons. Just more than a wee bit scary, I'd say. Two domino players sat grunting abuse at each other. At least I think it was abuse, hard to tell really. The one with the homemade tattoos and nose piercing seemed to be winning. This did not seem to please her opponent who appeared to belong to an as yet unclassified gender group.

It occurred to us that staring at anyone in this pub might not be such a good idea. It could get you into trouble, or, worse still, it could get you a new friend.

All of this, including the strange aroma hanging over the place could be overlooked if the beer had been up to scratch. It wasn't. Fifteen minutes after entering Sawney's we made our way back out, avoiding eye contact with our drinking companions.

Actually once we were away from the main street area, Saltcoats didn't look all that bad. Perhaps the re-developers had just run out of money before they reached it. Or perhaps,

like us, they had been there once and promised that they would
never, ever go back.
Our next pub, "Bobby's Bar", was much brighter and better
than "Sawney Beans". That really wouldn't take too much to
achieve, but it was really quite good. It was clean and
completely free of menacing characters. The beer was quite
good as well.

John: Our bus took us through Ardrossan, although you have
no idea where the three wee towns start and end-someone
should try and make one decent town out of the three of them.

As soon as you leave Ardrossan, you are going along the coast
passing beautiful scenery and great sea views. Arran and the
Cumbraes can be seen in the distance.

The bus took us up the hill into West Kilbride, which is much
larger than I thought it would be, although I have no idea why I
thought it would be tiny. It is up a hill in an out of the way
position, but it is very nice and we headed for *"The Tavern"*.
After an enjoyable, but up market priced pint, we decided to go
for a wander and find another pub. Before leaving, we asked
the barmaid where the nearest bus stop was, so we would know
when leaving the next pub. She came over to the door with us
and told us the stop was just to the right of the door, outside the
Chinese restaurant. There was no bus stop and no Chinese
Restaurant, unbelievable. We were going to go back in and
give us a piece of our minds, but we both realised that we don't
have much of our minds left, so we wandered up in the
direction we thought the bus stop might be.

Barmaid rating; ⬛⬛⬛ (she did talk to us after all)

We wandered up the road and found a nice looking pub called
"The Kings Arms" which was opposite the bus stop which was
next to a Chinese Restaurant. Either the barmaid in the Tavern
was mad or we don't listen to instructions. Considering all the
times we have screwed up, we believed we couldn't have
listened.

27

We wandered into the pub, which was reasonable and had a pint, don't remember the price, too many pubs visited already. The barman was very pleasant and I asked him why the town was at the top of a hill on a road to nowhere. His reply was that it had to be somewhere. I'm sure that's a line from a Dirty Harry movie. In my condition I couldn't think of a smart reply. You never can when you want to. West Kilbride is a nice place and worth a visit.

Barman Rating; 🅁🅁🅁

Craig: West Kilbride was a bit of a gamble as far as I was concerned. The last time I had been in a pub there was more than 35 years ago. I wasn't even sure that there were still pubs in the town. Many small rural pubs have closed down in the last few years. Some that I know around East Kilbride have either shut all together or only open at the weekend. Tragic! Happily there were two pubs in West Kilbride and they were both open. "The Tavern" and "The Kings Arms" supplied us

Craig's instinctive pub finding abilities
never desert him.

*with all we really needed; cold beer and a bit of friendly patter.
Who could ask for more?*
*Apart from a bit of mix up with the directions we were given to
our next bus stop everything went reasonably well in West
Kilbride. Even our bus turned up on time.*
John: Our next bus, with the same number as the last one, the
585, arrived on time, but I've no idea what time that was.
Funny I can remember bus numbers, but prices and time of day
are meaningless.
We had a nice run down the coast through Fairley, past Largs
Marina and Golf Course, with lovely views over to Millport
and then into Largs.
It was a nice, but cold evening. We went into our usual fish and
chip shop called *"The Viking"*. Craig had a fish and I had a
chicken supper. We wandered onto the front and had our
delicious suppers admiring the view across the Clyde estuary to
Cumbrae with Bute and Arran in the distance.
We still had a wee while before our train time so we went into
"Charlie Smiths". It's a nice wee pub on the front and we have
been in it several times before.
Barman Rating; 🍺🍺🍺
Finishing our pints we wandered up the main street to the
Station, bought our singles to East Kilbride (they were only
about £3, I think), and both slept the whole way to the Central
Station in Glasgow-magic.
*Craig: Once again we decided to dine in Largs. I'm convinced
that the best fish supper to be had in Western Scotland is to be
had in The Viking fish and chip shop, Largs.*
*And what better to wash down such a sumptuous meal than an
ice cold lager. "Charlie Smiths" is fast becoming a second
home to us. We always seem to end up there whenever we are
in Largs. Then again, maybe that's because it's next to the chip
shop.*

The journey up to Glasgow passed in a flash, for obvious reasons. Once in the station we decided that with 20 minutes to spare there was only one real option. After the swiftest of refreshments we experienced an equally swift journey back to EK.

John; Feeling refreshed, but too soon to be hung over, and having 20 minutes till the EK train, we nicked up into the Station Bar, don't know the name, and had a quick one.

On the train home to EK, I phoned Kate who offered to pick us up at the Monty at 10 o'clock. Thanks to the hours sleep on the Largs train, we were in control of our senses and knew this would give us an hour in the Monty-life doesn't get any better! A man sitting next to us was obviously listening to our conversation, because he said he heard us saying we were going to the Monty, where he was meeting a couple of his pals and could we show him the way. After slagging him off for listening to our conversation we said it would be no bother. That's the type of people we are.

Craig: *All that sleeping on the trains meant we were wide awake and more than ready for a quick night cap or two in "The Monty"*

Well that was the first journey of our latest tour completed. Against all the odds we had managed to survive a trip through the stranger parts of North Ayrshire. Hopefully the rest of our trips in the coming months will be a little more exciting, in the good sense of that word. It's hard to imagine that we will find any pubs worse than the two prize specimens we encountered today. But if they are out there then I'm sure we will find them. We have the knack.

John: So we went to the Monty, don't remember what we had, but ended up happy. Kate was waiting for us at 10, and so ended a great day out, even though some of the pubs and towns were instantly forgettable, if that is possible.

In Summary

The bar staff scores tell an interesting story on this first trip in our continuing journey around Scotland.

Things got off to a good start in Troon. The beer might have been a bit pricy but the service was pretty good. But that was short lived. There was a definite dip in service provision. Although the score went up in Irvine things were far from rosy. The barmaid in the 'Delta' managed to score quite highly, despite the fact that the pub was more than a little toxic. Perhaps there was a little bit of sympathy voting going on there.

The same kind of thing happened in our first pub in Saltcoats. The only reason the barman in 'Sawney Bean's' got such a high score was down to intimidation. One of the reviewers was feart fae him.

The rest of the pubs we visited were pretty much middle of the road. This helped bring up the days average score. Unfortunately it only brought it up to 2.44 out of 5 and into last place in our not very well thought out league table.

For our loyal readers, we feel this is not a trip for the faint hearted, unless you stay on the bus and bypass Saltcoats, although the beach might be nice.

Steamin' Doon the Clyde

(The River Clyde, the wonderful Clyde,
Where numpties and Nazis' live side by side.)

East Kilbride-Glasgow-Port Glasgow-Greenock
Gourock-Inverkip-Largs-Glasgow-East Kilbride

Steamin' Doon the Clyde

John; This was a journey that had everything from some of the worst, or most frightening pubs we have ever entered to some of the nicest places in Scotland that you could visit. Mind you, as it is the pubs we are interested in, the scenic side of things takes a back seat.

After the usual problems of having to get up reasonably early in the morning and getting the pieces made (the usual fillings), I kissed the wife goodbye with the usual promise of not drinking too much, aye right, and wandered down the hill to Craig's.

We started the journey on a completely new bus. It's a wee bright Orange bus. The bus number is the M1, which goes from the town centre in EK to Hairmyres Station. So instead of a 20 minute walk to the station in the village, or getting Irene to run us, or getting the bus into Glasgow, which is over an hour, we got this wee orange bus which took us to Hairmyres, which is the next station on the line, a new way to start the day-magic!

After a nice wee train journey into the Central Station, we wandered up to St. Vincent Street to wait for the McGill's 901, I think, to take us to Port Glasgow.

I never get fed up going into Glasgow in the morning to start a trip as all the other poor bastards are having to go to their work, if they are lucky enough to have a job.

We waited about 15minutes, and in that time about four buses passed going to Glasgow Airport. There was only about a total of six people on these buses. A great service for nobody. First moan of the day.

Craig; *After the first journey in our latest project went so well, we could hardly wait for our next expedition. A bus through the towns of Port Glasgow, Greenock and Gourock might not sound very exotic, and of course it wasn't. But it was very interesting.*

When we start out on one of our little adventures we usually have a fair idea of what we are likely to come across. As a couple of seasoned travellers, not to say, boozers, we have pretty much seen it all before.

Obviously we sometimes come across the odd surprise, the odd upset, but never anything outrageous or downright weird. That is until now.

Our trip along the south bank of The River Clyde and its estuary was a real eye opener. "You couldn't make it up", is an overused phrase these days, but it fits perfectly the description of our latest day out.

We decided to try a new bus service which would drop us off at Hairmyres Station. I was a little bit skeptical as there are other buses which would do the same thing. However, as soon as I saw it coming I knew we had made the right decision. It was a wee orange bus. Actually it was a very bright orange. There was no way we could miss seeing it coming. Given that old age is creeping up on us, the unkind among us might say cantering rather than creeping, we can use all the help we can get. I've noticed that as time goes by it gets harder and harder to make out the destination boards on the front of buses. That, as you can imagine, is a serious drawback to the professional bus traveller, especially if those travellers enjoy the occasional beer or two along the way. This new little 'High Viz' bus was a bit of a godsend for me. I just wonder if it would be possible to colour co-ordinate all of our buses.

When we got to the station John discovered he had left all of his carefully worked out itinerary sitting on his kitchen table. As ever he had produced an impressive spread sheet, detailing every aspect of our journey.

Copies had been made, filed and sent to interested parties. It was such a pity we never saw it again. Happily, as John has no embarrassment gene, he didn't even blush when he had to phone Kate to ask her where we were meant to be going and when we were supposed to catch our buses.

Steamin' Doon the Clyde

I suggested that in future maybe we could wear our timetables as little labels on our jackets. We could ask passing strangers to read them out to us, or better still, see us on to the right buses. I thought this was rather amusing. John didn't see the funny side of it though. Of course he is older than me so maybe it was too close to being necessary for him to be funny

John; Surprisingly, our McGill's bus arrived and we were happy to see that it was fairly quiet and it was a new bus, so no dried piss marks on the seats. But, like all McGill's buses, there was no padding on the seats, so it was a bumpy ride.

Even though I was not over enamoured about spending time in Port Glasgow, it was an enjoyable run down the side of the Clyde and the sun was shining. Everything looks better in the sun. We got off and wandered up into the main street and a nice surprise it was. The buildings are mostly built using a lovely red stone, might be sandstone, I have no idea, but the place looked nice. The pubs were another story.

The first place we looked into was called *"The Star Hotel"*. It was so bad and scary looking that Craig was too frightened to go in. Obviously it didn't bother me but to save Craig's blushes I suggested we go down to the bottom of the road to another pub called *"The Prince of Wales"*. That's how I remembered it anyway.

This was an old man's pub with a big, almost round bar. The place was badly needing a coat of paint, at the very least. A funny thing is that it had a juke box that must have been about 40 years old and really dusty. The next three pubs we visited all had identical ones. I found that really strange. Don't suppose anybody else did.

The barmaid was very nice and said she had worked in this bar for over 20 years and reckoned the biggest problem with the bar was the toilets. They had not been done up in the 20 years she had been there. They were really bogging. Don't think they had been flushed for the last 20 years! Mind you, it was a nice pub apart from the toilets, the barmaid was very nice and the beer was good. Being so early in the morning it was quiet but we didn't mind as we were sure the locals would be scary.

A pint on an empty stomach goes right to your head, if you know what I mean. We were only half way through them when we were talking about going back to *"The Star"*. We felt we had to go back as Craig would feel like a big nancy if we chickened out. The barmaid said one of the bars in *"The Star"* was a Celtic bar.

Craig; *The bus down to Port Glasgow was our old favourite, the McGill's 901. I have a major complaint with the makers of the latest models of buses and the McGill's ones in particular. The width of the seats is a constant source of annoyance for the both of us. They are apparently moulded for comfort, It seems clear to me that they used the vital statistics of the less fuller of figure among us when designing them. Anyone larger than an apprentice jockey would find it a struggle to fit themselves into a single seat. The only other explanation doesn't bear thinking about. Besides I'm big boned, apparently.*

We experienced a sense of relief, and a rush of blood to the nether regions, when we got off the torture machine in Port Glasgow. I was quite surprised how nice the place looked. That just shows how much I know.

Port Glasgow was once the main port on the Clyde. All imports to and exports from Glasgow had to come through the Port. The reason for this was quite simple. The River Clyde was too shallow for boats to navigate up river from that point until it was dredged in the mid-19th century. After that Port Glasgow's fortunes took a downward turn.

Speaking of downward turns, after a quick look about the place we spied our first watering hole of the day, 'The Star Hotel' The streets we had wandered round were made up from what seemed like quite imposing buildings and I had high hopes of a really classy first stop.

On closer inspection we realised our mistake. It was a bit grim on the outside and I wasn't convinced it was still operating as a pub. At first I couldn't even find the front door. We should have taken that as a sign. When I eventually did find the way in I suddenly wished I hadn't.

I opened the door a little and looked in. It was a complete midden. To be honest it looked like someone had thrown some old broken tables and chairs into a large dark cupboard. Several years' worth of dust had settled on every surface and electrical cables appeared to be stapled along the walls.

I turned to tell John I didn't fancy going in only to find he was legging it down the street. Without allocating any blame for choosing which pubs to visit we decided to replace "The Star Hotel" with a visit to "The Prince of Wales" which was only a couple of hundred yards down the road. Like the present holder of that job, "The Prince of Wales" has seen better days.

Actually, from the outside it looks not too bad. I imagine that's where the entire maintenance budget went. Inside hasn't seen a paint brush this side of the millennium.

Apart from the ubiquitous flat screen telly, the newest thing in the bar was the juke box which first saw action in the early 70's. Take these two items out and you've got a 1900's film set. There's hardly a hint of colour in the place. Good pint though, and a very pleasant barmaid.

While knocking back our beers we managed to talk ourselves into going back up the road to "The Star Hotel". It's a man thing.

Barmaid Rating; 🍺🍺🍺 *(for overcoming the lavy problem).*

John; Having visited Larkhall we felt it was only fair to see if a Celtic bar in Port Glasgow was as mental as the Rangers one in Larkhall. So back up the road we went and into *"The Star"*. What a dump. When we stood at the bar you could feel the floor sagging. There were two locals having a pint and they roared to the barman who was down in the other bar. This must have been the Celtic bar as when you looked down the stairs you could see a huge tri-colour.

This guy came up the stairs. He looked like the toughest man in the world. He wore a tee shirt with no sleeves, but you could not see any skin as they were covered in tattoos. The only word I could make out was Celtic, but I was frightened to look too closely as he might have asked what I was looking at.

Having said that, he was very friendly and so were the two locals. They had no heavy beer, only Lager, but he offered to clean the pipes and put on a new barrel. I ordered a Lager. I am as big a shit bag as Craig.

'Abandon all hope ye who enter here'.
(Yes it was pretty hellish.)

We enjoyed our pints and after humming the chorus to Athenry, which is a great tune, we wandered out into the sunshine.

Although the pub was in very poor repair and it was a Celtic pub, the barman and the atmosphere in the pub were great. He also told us we held a tune well.

Craig; *I pushed the door of the Star mausoleum open and went in. It was even worse than we thought it would be.*

I could hear voices but couldn't see their owners. My first thought was that the place was haunted by some less than discerning ghosts. However, the noise was coming from round the corner. In the bar two old men, both well over 70, were sitting at a table chatting away. As far as I could tell they were the youngest thing in the place. The floor boards moved under the lino as we walked in. It might have been a money saving exercise, but I really do feel that it would be much safer to actually nail the floorboards down rather than depend on gravity to hold them in place. The bar itself seemed to be made from a variety of wood types, including orange box and balsa wood. There were some gaping holes in it, perhaps evidence of some heated debates in the past. The walls, and for that matter everything else, were stained nicotine brown. To be honest, the whole place looked like a sepia photograph of Steptoe's scrap yard.

Not that I'd say a word against the place to the barman. Actually I was trying very hard not to catch his eye never mind speak to him. Usually if we are not served immediately we get quite vocal, not in the Star Hotel we didn't. I've never met the man but I'm convinced that there is never an ounce of bother in the pub when he is on duty.

Right enough it would be hard to imagine the two old geezers we met in there getting up to any high jinx.

Usually I would comment on the beer we had but to be quite honest I couldn't concentrate on the taste of it for looking round about myself. I did think about taking a photograph but my hands were shaking too much. Besides, I doubt there was enough light in the place to get a picture.

Outside we found the door into the other bar room, "The Celtic Bar". The bloke standing in the doorway didn't seem very friendly as he stared through us so we kept moving.

Barman Rating; ▨▨▨▨▨ *(couldn't give this bloke any less)*

John; We wandered down the road toward the bus station and Craig was really amused by a Chinese Restaurant with the name *"The Fan King"*. He said you could imagine some guy saying to his wife, 'I am away down to the Fanking Restaurant, OK'. His wife would probably say 'who are you fanking kidding, you're away to the fanking pub'.

So apart from the pubs needing a bit of TLC, Port Glasgow was a nice wee town which should be highlighted in the Scottish Tourist Brochures-a place you will not forget-with a great fanking restaurant.

So it was back down to the bus station for the 10 minute journey along the Clyde to Greenock.

Arriving in brilliant sunshine, we wandered along the road and without spending much time exploring the town, went into a pub on the main street called *"Legends"*. It might be a legend in its own mind, but it did nothing for Craig and me. It was neither an old man's pub or modern. I imagine it was opened in the 80s' and inside it looked like someone's badly furnished living room. Even with the 70s jukebox it lacked atmosphere. It was like a lounge bar. The only thing that made it memorable were two guys at the bar who were in their 40s or 50s, looked like twins and were having a heated discussion about whether shaving cream should be Fusion or not Fusion. This went on for ages and we had no idea what they were talking about. Talk about a couple of nancies. We finished our pints and were glad to be back outside in the sunshine. Never saw the barman after we got our pints. We assumed he was away shaving.

Craig; I had high hopes for Greenock even though I'd never actually stopped there for a drink. Given what we had just experienced it was a pretty safe bet that our next pub would be an improvement.

It was, but only just. "Legends" was not quite what we were expecting. With a name like that you would think there must be some sort of theme to the place, unless the theme was a bus station waiting room I think the designers missed their mark. It was just a big bare room where someone, not necessarily a craftsman, had built a big square bar. Usually I enjoy the daft conversations you hear in pubs, but this place was just too bizarre. Less said the better I think. We got the next bus out of town and on to Gourock. **Barman rating;**

A terrible misuse of the word 'Legends'.
Well-quipped bus shelter might be more apt.

John; As Greenock did not look very inviting, we wandered back over to the bus station and after eating a couple of my corned beef pieces, got on another McGill's bus. No idea of the number. We reckoned the sooner we got to Gourock the better. As soon as you get into the outskirts of Gourock, the houses are bigger and look as if they are worth a few bob.

However, we wanted to visit real pubs so got off the bus in the centre of the town just about opposite the railway station and went into a pub called *"The Old Wherry"*. A big blond and very cheery barman made us feel very welcome and we started to have a great chat with him and a wee old couple who were sitting at a table near us. It was a very nice pub with great atmosphere and a great barman.

Everything seemed perfect, the best pub we had visited for ages. As in all good pub discussions, the conversation turned to politics, my right wing views went down well with the barman, if not Craig. Things started to get a bit strange when, after annoying Craig by praising Mrs. Thatcher to the heavens, he started telling Craig about how good Hitler had been as a leader. Craig was sure he seemed serious, and this was proved to be the case when after a heated discussion with Craig on Hitler's many virtues, he disappeared behind the bar and re-appeared with a Nazi cap and armband with Swastika.

When he saw that nobody was laughing, he said that he only kept them for a joke. I felt it a bit strange the items were so close at hand. Funnily enough, when you looked at him, he was the spitting image of what a relative of a Nazi might look like, big, heavy and blond. Even his hair was combed in the style of Hitler, although he did not have the moustache. I found it all fairly funny in a strange way. Craig, on the other hand, was on the verge of invading Poland (or the other side of the bar).

That wasn't the end of people acting like Nazi bastards.

Craig; *This was one town I definitely knew a bit about. We have been there quite often on our travels and have enjoyed a beer or two while we were at it. This time though we decided to try a pub we hadn't visited before. It was quite random really. We got off the bus and there it was, the "Old Wherry". It looked very neat, very orderly you might say.*

We have found that many pubs nowadays are less than friendly to strangers. They tend to look after their regulars first and foremost, not so in the Old Wherry. Almost as soon as we pushed the door open the barman was chatting away to us. That's always a good sign, well almost always. Through all the general nonsense that gets talked in pubs I noticed that in this one the landlord was doing most of the talking. What was really annoying was that he was agreeing with John an awful lot. This was a bit of an omen. John gets the Daily Mail delivered to his home, quite openly, not even in a plain wrapper. It's a bit of a worry when he finds someone who agrees with his outlook on life.

Even he was a bit stunned by our new pal Ted's views. At one point he proclaimed to the entire bar, all four of us, that his pub was the only place in Gourock where a man could speak his mind. I began to suspect he meant only if it happened to be a warped mind. Very soon we got onto politics, a subject usually banned in all pubs. I suggested that his politics seemed to be a bit to the right of Adolph Hitler. This comparison seemed to please him quite a bit. Some people just refuse to be insulted. I decided my best, and safest, bet was to play along and humour him. The best I could come up with was that at least he'd got the trains to run on time. There was no stopping him after that. He argued that Hitler had not only been the victim of some bad press, but that he had been a good leader for Germany and we could all learn from him. I reminded him of the Second World War, among other things, but he wouldn't be put off. He then disappeared through the back only to return with some Nazi regalia, including a swastika armband. I think he saw the look on our faces and tried to make out it was just

for a bit of a laugh. It's like I've always said, those bloody Germans have no sense of humour. He was kidding nobody.
The thing that struck me was he reminded me of someone. Maybe it was the blond hair and the blue eyes, I don't know. I thought about asking him if he'd ever been to Brazil when he was a boy but I didn't think he would appreciate that.
Having had a couple of lagers by this time we decided to say aufwiedersehen to Fuhrer Ted's Beer Keller. We made a strategic withdrawal to the nearest friendly bar. I acted as a rearguard to let John escape before me. At least we didn't have to tunnel our way out.
We made our way along the road, keeping a wary eye out for camp guards.

Barman Rating; **John-**🍺🍺🍺🍺; *Craig* 🍺

John; We left the bar, (I goose stepped out the door), and wandered along towards the bus stop. As I looked behind, expecting to see a panzer division coming along the front of Gourock, our next bus came into sight.

As we approached the bus stop, the bus was passing so I stuck out my arm to let the driver know we were coming for the bus. The bastard stopped for half a second to let a man off, then buggered off without waiting the two seconds to let us on. Is Gourock full of Nazi bastards, or were we just unlucky?

To be honest, neither of the incidents bothered us at all and we wandered into the pub next to the bus stop called *"The Kemrock"*. It's funny how when you get to be our age, even Nazis infiltrating Gourock is not a major issue. Mind you, it would be great if they had power over bus drivers who do not stop to pick you up.

Unlike the other pubs we were in, there was very little to report from this pub. It was uninspiring, yet there was nothing wrong with it other than, for the second time today, you couldn't get a pint of heavy or 70 shilling. I had lager again and halfway through it I started to get a horrible smell from the glass. The lager tasted alright. I asked the barman to pour it into a clean glass. To be fair, he offered me another pint, but to Craig's amazement, I said a new glass would be fine. Think I didn't want to be beholden to this barman in case he was a friend of the previous barman and a member of the Fourth Reich and put me on a hit list.

We asked the barman if he knew our friend from the previous pub and he said something along the lines of since he took over the pub many of the regulars stopped going into it. Think he only wanted people in uniform.

This pub also had an old juke box. I like old juke boxes and also music of the 60s' and 70s'. Sandy Shaw was a great favourite of mine. Think I am starting to wander a bit in this story.

Craig; Once inside our next pub "The Kepoch" we felt a bit safer. That being said they did try to poison John's beer. We chatted to two customers in the bar about what had happened in the Wherry. They were not surprised. One of them told us that most of the original customers had moved out when the new Fuhrer took over. The Kepoch itself is a fairly reasonable pub. It's bright and quite modern and when they're not poisoning their customers, the beer is more than passable.

Barman Rating; R R R

Inverkip was our next stop. The difference between this village pub and the best Gourock had to offer was astonishing.

"The Elbow Room" is part of the Inverkip Hotel. The clever middle class name annoyed me as did the tasteful middle class decor. I'm surprised they didn't have a tradesman's entrance. The barman looked a little shell shocked when we ordered an entire pint of beer each. I can imagine things really hot up at the weekends, when the Mensa quiz gets the pulses racing. It was the kind of place where, after three or four brews, I could quite easily turn into Rab C Nesbit.

Actually I was still a bit annoyed by our earlier session in Gourock. The Elbow Room is a very nice little country pub.

The Inverkip Hotel. It's just as neat and tidy on the inside. Not exactly oor cup of tea then, you might be forgiven for saying.

John; I think McGill's have a monopoly of the routes in this area cause it was one of them that turned up to take us to our next port of call, Inverkip. Getting on the bus, I thanked the driver for stopping and letting us on. He said nothing.

It's a lovely run down the front at Gourock, passed the Cloch Lighthouse and round the coast to Inverkip.

When you get off the bus it looks like a wee town with only a main road, a couple of shops and a hotel (with a pub, or lounge bar), but up the back towards the railway line are hundreds of new and fairly new houses. There is also a huge marina down at the front, where marinas are usually found. I think Inverkip has thousands of people who commute to Glasgow and other places. Mind you, there is very little work in these places, so who knows what all the locals do.

The bar in the *"Inverkip Hotel"* is very nice in an up market way, all wood, brass and malt whiskies. Nobody spoke to us. The people were in groups wearing up-market casual clothes. Each to their own I say. The bar staff obviously knew we were not of their class and the only boat we had been on was The Waverley, They were right.

Barman Rating; █ *(snobs)*

Craig; *Largs once again was our final destination. We decided to change our usual watering hole and so after another gourmet fish supper, "Macaulays" bar was the lucky recipient of our slightly sozzeled company.*

I'm sure we had a rare old time but lack of sleep meant I lost all memory of our visit. A good sleep on the train up to Glasgow fully refreshed me and John too, I would imagine.

Lucky for us we met Kate and her friend Liz in Central Station. If we hadn't met up with them we might have been forced to knock back another drink of two.

So having saved a bit of cash we headed straight for the train.

Back in EK the girls insisted we go to the "Monty" for a couple of drinks. We were a bit tired from all our travels but didn't want to disappoint them so we agreed to go in.

It was a nice way to end our latest adventure and gave us time to reflect on what a strange day we had experienced.

We were glad to have completed that stretch of the Clyde Estuary but, we now had a couple more pubs to put on our list of places whose doors we will never darken again.

John; We downed our pints and headed out to the main street to await the next McGill's coach. All McGill's coaches seem to be the same. They are very low and bumpy and not very comfortable. I think they are made for relatively short journeys and Mr. McGill has no thought for older peoples' arses.

Steamin' Doon the Clyde

Anyway, the arse rattler turned up to take us to Wemyss Bay where we had only a couple of minutes to change buses to take us to our final destination, Largs. As we approached Wemyss Bay, our next bus was in front of us causing Craig and I to panic. All was well as we passed the other bus and managed to make a quick change in Wemyss Bay. If we had missed the changeover we would have had to spend 40 minutes in the *"Station Bar"* on the pier. Just as well this didn't happen as I would have wanted to jump on the next ferry to Rothesay, my favourite place (apart from Las Vegas).

As you know we have visited Largs before and the only reason for being there on this trip was to get the train back to Glasgow. But we still had time to have a fish supper and a pint in *"Macaulay's"*. Got to get your priorities right.

For the second trip in a row we both slept all the way to Glasgow Central, a great way to travel a journey you know well.

As we waited to board our train back to EK, I got a tap on the shoulder. It was the wife with her pal Liz. They had been in town having a facial (Liz had given Kate a voucher for her birthday). A facial scrub, as it is called, is supposed to take away all their wrinkles and make their faces all smooth. My suggestion that they should get arseules didn't go down to well. Amazing how brave you are with a bevy in you.

Fortunately they had a good bucket in them and took it in the spirit it was made!

So we travelled with the girls on the train back to EK. This is not in the spirit of our travelling rules and Craig was not too pleased until the girls suggested we all go to the Monty for a few pints-what girls, and lucky ones too.

Liz's husband Jim joined us in the Monty and we had a great end to the day.

Got home about 11.30pm and straight to bed-magic!

In Summary

Today's little trip will possibly go down as the scariest day out we've ever had.

It is doubtful that we have ever seen a place as run down as the bar we had a drink in down in Port Glasgow, not in real life anyway. Possibly on the Discovery Channel who are forever broadcasting documentaries on urban decay.

The differences between this place and the one down in Greenock were quite strange. In Greenock the pub was fairly modern and had all its fixtures and fittings attached, securely, in their proper places. What it didn't have was any sort of atmosphere.

The pub up in Port Glasgow has plenty of atmosphere. Unfortunately it is a menacing one.

The first pub in Gourock took the biscuit for oddness. Having the hair on the back of your neck standing on end for the entire duration of our visit to this place was an unusual experience.

But a trip doon the Clyde is an easy and great day out. Just try some different pubs.

Blitzed in Clydebank

(The Germans failed to waste it all.
But the planners succeeded by building that mall)

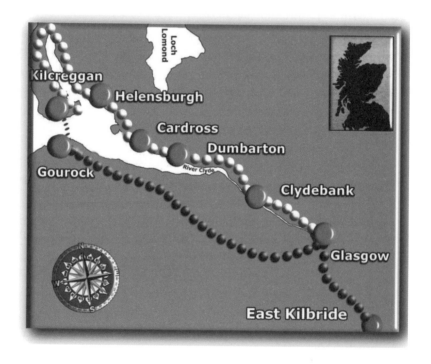

*East Kilbride-Glasgow-Clydebank-Dumbarton
Cardross-Helensburgh-Kilcreggan-Gourock
Glasgow-East Kilbride*
(Seven Buses, Three Trains, One Ship)

Blitzed in Clydebank

John; Another glorious day awaited the third trip in our latest drunken adventure. I was looking forward to this trip as it took in a lot of places and we would be on buses, trains and a ship. Only problem with this type of trip is that it is only the buses that are free.

The areas we were travelling in were similar to our first two trips in that some of the stopping places were not the most upmarket in Scotland. Having said that, these are the places where the pubs are the best and the people are most like us, drunks.

After waving goodbye to Kate in glorious sunshine, I walked down to Craig's house which is almost next to the bus stop. I was five minutes early so had to wait while Irene got Craig ready for the day, pieces and all.

When planning the route on the computer, though god knows why I bother, I realised that the number 66 bus would take us from EK straight to Clydebank. When I say straight, it goes through Glasgow, along Great Western Road and god knows where else before arriving at Clydebank, almost two hours later.

We decided instead to get the 201 bus from outside Craig's house to Hairmyres Station, the train into Glasgow and the bus from Argyll Street to Clydebank. This is actually quicker and a more comfortable way to travel, although it costs 60p on the train into Glasgow. Not much when you consider the 10 or so pints we would probably consume later.

So we made our way into Glasgow and came out of the Central Station at "The Highlandman's Umbrella". I think there's a teuchter way of spelling it. It's called that because a lot of the teuchters used to meet there years ago on their first visit from the highlands and islands. Most of them to became cops, and what great cops they made, every one over six feet six and hard as nails.

Blitzed in Clydebank

We now have wee men and girls in police uniforms cycling about the streets-what's that all about?

Craig; Today was the day we were to finish the last section of our journey along the River Clyde. Much as I love the country's most famous river, I was really glad to be finishing this part of the country.

It's not that it has been uninteresting or even uneventful, it's just that it has taken us a lot of time to cover quite a short stretch of coastline.

This journey's list of destinations contained three places which were entirely new to me. Clydebank, Dumbarton and Cardross didn't sound much like tourist hotspots to me, and for once I was right about something. Not that we consider ourselves to be tourists of course. The fact is I was convinced that John had just made up Cardross.`

We had spent a lot of time choosing our destinations for this latest trip. Why we included Clydebank on this list is still a bit of a mystery to me it has to be said. I have never, to the best of my knowledge, ever even passed through this place before.

One of the few things I knew about it was that it had been blitzed by the Germans during the Second World War. Another was that it very obviously sat on the banks of the Clyde. The only other interesting fact I knew about the place was that it boasted an incredibly unsuccessful football team. Armed with all this knowledge I wasn't particularly looking forward to our visit.

John; We walked along Argyle Street and had a look at the timetables posted up on the shelters at the bus stops.

Clydebank was not as prominently mentioned as I would have thought. The timetable people don't realise that the place has been rebuilt since the wartime bombings by the Germans.

After a few minutes a bus came along, I have forgotten the number, and we got on.

Blitzed in Clydebank

I'm getting worse. Instead of putting my bus pass on the wee place for scanning, I put my debit card on it. This pantomime was repeated another twice during the day. There's something wrong with me.

When the bus started I got up and asked the driver to give us a shout when we were about the centre of Clydebank. In traditional non helpful mode he said Clydebank didn't have a centre. I assumed the Luftwaffa had destroyed it. That was the end of that conversation.

We kept an eye on the road as we passed along through places like Partick, Whiteinch and Yoker before passing a sign saying Clydebank Town Centre. Aren't our bus drivers wonderful?

So we got off the bus, thanking the driver, as most people do now, though god knows why.

Clydebank, an industry free zone.

Blitzed in Clydebank

The sun was shining, so the place looked nice as we wandered along the main road looking for craters or other signs of the war. But everything seemed ok, except for the buildings the Germans missed. Only kidding.

We went down a side street to see if we could get a look at the river which made Clydebank famous and after a climb up onto a wall, saw the river, and a huge crane in the distance. It all looked very dramatic in the sunshine.

The main reason for all this wandering about was that we had arrived at 10.35am, so we had nearly half an hour to kill before the pubs opened.

As opening time approached, we wandered along the main road looking for a pub, and low and behold we found one, called *"The Park Bar"*. And what a nice bar it was. A good atmosphere and spotless, without the smell of bleach that some pubs have because they pour it on the floor to make you think they've cleaned the place.

The walls had pictures of some of the great ships that have been buildt there. One of the ships was called "The Battleaxe". Probably named in honour of wives throughout Clydebank.

We had an enjoyable first pint of the day there and a wee chat with the barmaid who said she had worked there for about 10 years. When I told her what we were doing and that we were going to be in Dumbarton next, she gave us a strange look but then told us she lived there and gave us the names of a couple of good pubs in the town-old men's pubs she said. We didn't take offence as we are old.

So out we went, said goodbye to Clydebank and got on our next bus. I think it was a 216, to take us to Dumbarton.

Barmaid Rating; 🍺🍺🍺

Craig; While waiting for our bus at the stop in Argyll Street we speculated about what we would find in Clydebank. There were a few bad taste jokes about the Luftwaffa doing its level best to redevelop the town.

Blitzed in Clydebank

It was decided that, since we were strangers to the area, it would be a good idea to ask our bus driver to let us off in the town centre. The driver, not the friendliest person I've come across, managed to grunt out the response "Clydebank disnae hiv a toon centre". John, in all innocence, I think, asked, "Is that down to all they Germans?"

On first impression I wasn't very impressed. Even though it was a sunny day things didn't look too good. It was quite easy to imagine what the place would look like on a dreich, overcast or rainy day. I could almost taste the depression. Then again bus stations do tend to be a bit on the rough side, so perhaps we were not seeing the town at its best. With a little time to spare, that's to say pre-opening time we strolled down towards the riverside. That turned out to be harder than we imagined. We couldn't find the damned thing. After a bit of a search, John announced he could see it, but I wasn't convinced. We could see one of the giant cranes in the distance so it had to be close by.

The whole area seemed to be an industry free zone. We wondered if the barren land along the river was perhaps under re-development or maybe no-one had got round to building anything after the Germans had paid their last visit. My preferred theory is that this part of Scotland, like so many other areas had been industrially cleansed by Maggie Thatcher and her storm troopers.

Anyway it was getting hot and we were getting thirsty. We needed to find a pub. And what a great pub we found. "The Park Bar" was a really well appointed watering-hole. It was as clean as any pub I've ever seen. All of the brass work, of which there was plenty, was glistening. The bar and the tables were also spotless. Best of all, the barmaid was very pleasant. Even after John had given her the benefit of his patter she continued to smile and chat away. That's sheer professionalism in my book.

We could quite easily have stayed for another drink but we were men on a mission and our dedication drove us on.

John; I found this part of the journey very enjoyable. We passed through Dalmuir, Old Kilpatrick, went under the Erskine Bridge, and past the start of the Forth and Clyde Canal at Bowling. All these places looked very nice, and it would have been great if we had the time to get off and explore them in more detail, or visit more pubs. You see a lot of places using local buses that you miss if you're on a train or driving on the main roads. Buses are great, even if the drivers are sometimes a bit of a letdown.

We arrived in Dumbarton about 12 noon and had a wander down to the river Leven which flows through the town. The sun was still shining and we sat on a bench at the side of the river and had our pieces. I had Sandwich Spread and cheese instead of my beloved Corned Beef, but they were great none the less.

We parked ourselves here for a well deserved pint.

Craig had brought his big camera-the the one he took his prize winning shot of Arran which is now the cover of Millport's 2011 Calendar-work that out if you can.

We took a couple of shots of the scenic grandeur. I usually just take photos of the pubs we go into so I can look at them remember where we have been, but even I was moved to take a couple of snaps of the river. The only downside of the river was it was full of old boats of all shapes and sizes. The only thing they had in common was that none of them looked seaworthy, they were all wrecks. I think it was a boat graveyard, and it spoiled the overall look of the place which was really nice.

It is unusual for Craig and I to waste time looking at scenic grandeur during opening hours. We must be getting soft in our even older age.

Pieces and photos finished, we wandered into *"The Lennox"*, or the Bobby as we called it, assuming it must be, or was owned by the legendry Bobby Lennox, a Celtic great. I kept an eye out for him but as I have no idea what he would look like now, or even if the poor guy is still alive, my chances were remote. This was one of the pubs the barmaid in *"The Park Bar"* had said was good. The only complaint I could make was the number of huge tellies that were hanging on the walls. There must have been about five in what was a fairly small pub. One small telly for the racing is enough for any pub that you want to go in to for a chat or a read of the paper.

The pints were ok although I think my mouth was rotten as all of the pints so far tasted slightly off. I'm sure it was me. The barmaid was very chatty with the locals and seemed to be very knowledgeable about all the sports that were being shown. I like that.   **Barmaid Rating;** R R R

We finished our pints and wandered along the street about 100 yards to the second pub we had been told was good. This one was called *"The Burgh Bar"*.

This was more like an old man's pub, it was fairly busy and there was only one telly so you could hear yourself talk, although what Craig and I are saying after about four pints is usually not worth listening to. There was a great dog in the place, I think it was a spaniel of sorts, and very friendly.

We enjoyed our pints and everyone in the pub had a friend to talk to, so nobody spoke to us. That's ok with me, although some local patter can be very funny at times.

The service was good but the barman was busy talking to his regulars, but as he served us as soon as we came in I cannot make any bad comments about him.

Barman rating; 🍺🍺🍺 (that's just a guess, he might be better than that)

Old wreck simply rusting away. The boats are in pretty bad nick as well.

Blitzed in Clydebank

Craig; We didn't have far to go to catch our next bus and it came along quite quickly. John stepped forward to get on the bus waving what he thought was his bus pass. Once again it was his debit card he was holding. I suggested he might try his electricity bill the next time. They say you should never laugh at your own jokes and I suffered for doing just that. As I turned, still laughing, I tripped off the kerb and nearly launched myself, head first, into the bus. God knows what the driver thought he was getting on his bus. I have to stress that we had only had one pint at this stage. Things didn't bode well for the rest of the trip.

The run down to Dumbarton didn't take long. To be honest, I wouldn't have known we were in Dumbarton if John hadn't told me.

For a change we decided not to go straight to the pub and instead strolled round to the banks of the river Leven. It was really very nice. There were a lot of old boats tied up in midstream. I love boats, old or new. John was not as impressed as I was by the boats. He said that these old wrecks shouldn't be allowed to just sit there. I said he might be in big trouble if they suddenly decided to drag away all the old wrecks sitting in that area. Once again he wasn't amused.

After a couple of sandwiches we walked back round to the main street and entered "The Lennox Bar". The outside of the pub didn't look too promising, but inside it was quite bright and friendly. It was also a bit noisy. There must have been at least five big flat screen tellies on as well as a very loud jukebox. It was as if they were trying to get their money's worth out of all their expensive technology. The barmaid was quite chatty and seemed to know an awful lot about football.

Actually knowing a lot more about football than me would not be too hard a skill to achieve. She insisted on telling us, and anyone else who would listen, all about the chances of Scottish teams playing in Europe. Apparently they didn't have any. Not wishing to show my total lack of knowledge in these matters I did a lot of nodding and shaking of the head, hoping I was doing it at the correct moments.

"The Burgh Bar" was a very different experience. It was a right "old geezers" pub, all drab wood paneling and subdued lighting. To be honest I think the lighting might have been subdued by the build-up of stoor on the lamp shades. Whatever the reason for the lighting effects, it suited us well. If they'd only had a couple of comfortable bar stools for us it would have been perfect.

John; I nicked out and tried to phone my pal big Dave who lives in Cardross, our next port of call, to see if he wanted to join us. There was no answer so I assumed he must be on the golf course or on holiday. Both were very possible. I also sent him a text, but at time of writing this I have had no answer so I'll give him a day or two and call again. People of our age never know how to retrieve messages or other high tech stuff.

So we got on our next bus, a 206 again. We had a very pleasant run along the shores of the Clyde to Cardross. Most people who live here are loaded. All the houses are pretty flash.

We wandered into *"The Coach House Inn"*, which is across the road from the clubhouse of Cardross Golf Club where Dave spends most of the year.

It is a very nice pub, in an up market sort of way. When we walked in the lady behind the bar (not a barmaid type of girl) asked if we were eating today. We said no, we were drinking. So she showed us through the back, away from the posh people, to the public bar, which was still pretty up market. After giving us our pints, I think she was still a bit worried by the look of us 'cause she told us there was a very nice Beer Garden out the side of the bar.

So we took the hint and wandered out into the sun and enjoyed a couple of pints in the sunshine. I kept looking over to see if Dave was coming off the course, and even shouted over to a guy, who was not Dave. Thank god he never heard me. Never mind.

"The Coach House" is a very nice place, and I can imagine very popular with the locals for meals, wine and gin and tonics. I still feel Craig and I could have fitted in no bother if we had dressed up a wee bit. Mind you, we don't look classy.

Barmaid Rating;  (a bit stuck up, but never mind it's a flash place)

John searches for the tradesmen's entrance at the Coach House Inn, Cardross.

We were covering this part of the coast very well and our next bus, the 216 again (there must be hundreds of them), took us along the Clyde and into Helensburgh. We had planned just to get the next bus right away, but a combination of Craig needing the toilet and the fact that we had missed it anyway made up our minds. It was off to find a toilet with a bar attached.

"The Royal Bar" on the front fitted the bill and in we went for a piss and a pint. It was a nice wee pub and the locals seemed friendly, although this being Helensburgh, some of them would have been tourists. They were mostly old guys, probably in for a pint while the wife wandered round the tourist shops.

The barman was friendly and helpful and gave us directions to find our bus. This is more than most bus drivers would do.

Barman Rating; 🍺🍺🍺

Craig; We arrived in Cardross and once again I had to depend on John to tell me where we were. I really need to research these things more carefully.

"The Coach House Inn" looked a bit too up-market for my liking. It was very much your country inn type of place. We managed to enter the wrong door and were met by a well-dressed and well-spoken young lady. She immediately clocked that we were neither of these things and ushered us into the bar area. We then impressed her so much with our patter that she suggested we might like to take our drinks outside. I prefer to think she meant that we should go out to the beer garden but you never know.

Outside we sat admiring the view across the road. The Cardross Golf Club is very probably a fairly exclusive club, but it is far from well designed. To the untrained eye it looks like it was modeled on something built by a Blue Peter presenter. These guys could do wonders with margarine tubs, pipe cleaners and sticky backed plastic.

We had a while to wait for our next bus so we decided to make Cardross a two pint stop. The classy young lady in the bar graciously allowed John back indoors long enough to order another round.

Helensburgh was our next stop. Originally we were not going to have a beer here but by now John had the taste. "The Royal

Bar" was quite a reasonable wee pub with very few distinguishing features. It did have a working toilet and that made it very special for us both.

John; After a pint and a last minute visit to the toilet, we wandered up the road to catch the 16.05pm bus to Kilcreggan. This is a journey we have done before. We went up past the Nuclear Submarine base, with the protesters not protesting, then round Garelochhead to finish up at Kilcreggan.

We have been in 'The Lighthouse' before and Craig was looking forward to meeting up with the owner, the lovely, and loud, Liz, with whom Craig had his photo taken on our last visit. So we were disappointed when there was no sign of her. I suppose everyone deserved a day off now and then.

But the day was still glorious, so we sat outside in the sunshine and enjoyed our pints while admiring the scenery over the Clyde estuary.

A quiet, cool pint, with a great view of the car park.

Blitzed in Clydebank

We are lucky to live in such a nice place, I just wish everyone who comes into contact with the public and tourists would cheer up a bit. Not all of them mind you, Liz, who I just mentioned was one of the cheeriest people Craig and I have ever met. Maybe she's been arrested by the tourist board for being too nice to people.

Barman Rating; ▓▓▓ (would have been 5 if Liz had been in)

Craig; The Lighthouse" in Kilcreggan is a place we both know well. We'd been there before and I wasn't too happy to be paying it another visit, but John insisted. Given what I'd said about the proprietor in our first book, I wasn't too keen on a reunion. Just to wind me up a bit John had threatened to bring along a copy of the book to show to her. As it turned out he'd forgotten to bring the book so, with no incriminating evidence, I was in the clear. Liz, the owner, wasn't on duty anyway so all that worry for nothing, just typical.

As it was such a nice day we decided to go all continental and sit outside to drink our beer while taking in the scenery. Unfortunately most of the scenery was suddenly blotted from view by the front of a very large four by four truck which drove up and parked two feet away from my nose. The driver found it quite humorous when I suggested he find somewhere else to leave his monster truck. I probably wouldn't have minded quite so much if he had actually been a customer of the pub, but he just wandered off down the street. As it was I just settled for a quiet seethe.

Although I had dodged the bullet by not meeting up with the owner of the pub, I was a bit worried about getting onto the little boat over to Gourock. The last time we'd been on it harsh words had been exchanged between me and the ticket collector. Well my words had been harsh, his had been unintelligible. This time I went to great lengths to make sure that it would be John who bought the tickets. Once again I had been worrying for nothing. It was a different crew.

John; We watched as our next mode of transport, the wee boat that ploughs between Gourock, Kilcreggan and Helensburgh all day made its way over to get us. After boarding and paying our couple of quid for the sail over, we went out the back and enjoyed the 10 minute or so sail to Gourock in glorious weather.

Craig was a bit nervous getting on the boat as the last time we were on it he lost his ticket and ended up nearly throwing a wee Polish guy overboard for asking for the ticket as he got off. It was the wee Polish guy who sold it to Craig in the first place. What a laugh that was.

We enjoyed our fish suppers sitting on the front in Gourock before boarding the train to Glasgow Central. As usual, we always try to get a train back to Glasgow as the buses, although free, don't have toilets, and as usual, we slept all the way and never needed the toilet. Typical, almost three pounds down the toilet!

We got on the train to EK and Craig decided that we would get off at Hairmyres. This is our new way of doing the last part of the journey home-if it works.

The 201 bus that would take us to *"The Lum"* didn't show and we had to walk a long way (Craig obviously said it was no distance at all) and we got the 66 to *"The Crooked Lum"* (which is its proper name). This is the pub at the roundabout, about three minute walk from our houses, so after a couple in there we wandered up the road in relative sobriety. The reason for this happening was that we had had no alcohol from boarding the wee boat in Kilcreggan at about 5.30pm till arriving at *"The Lum"* at about eight o'clock. Kate was surprised and a bit suspicious. Why was I sober? There you go; they're never happy.

Craig; *Over in Gourock we resisted the urge to down a cool pint or two and opted for a fish supper instead. We must be getting old.*

Blitzed in Clydebank

The journey up to Glasgow Central Station was pretty routine. Par for the course, we got off the train and walked what seemed like miles to the main departure board only to find our train to East Kilbride had been sitting next to the one we had just got off.

On the train I suggested to John that instead of rounding off the night in "The Monty", we could make our way to "The Crooked Lum".

It seemed like a good idea but, as ever, things didn't work out entirely to plan. The bus we were supposed to catch at the station didn't turn up and of course John managed to blame me for that. There was nothing else for it but to walk a few hundred yards to another bus stop. To listen to John you would think he had been force marched along The West Highland Way. Obviously we did make it to the Lum but not when and in the way we thought.

Ending our day's travel so close to home meant we didn't need to call on anyone to give us a lift up the road, which was just as well really as no one had volunteered their services.

"...an she definitely said *this* was the Beer Garden?"

In Summary

Clydebank isn't the most picturesque place we have ever visited. In fact it could well be the bleakest. In its defence we believe it is going through a period of redevelopment.

The more callous among us might suggest that the process began in the early 1940s and the local authorities have been dragging their feet ever since in their efforts to come up with a completion date.

That would be so wrong. Obviously the decline in heavy industry is to blame for Clydebank's current predicament. And we all know who's to blame for that, do we not Mrs. Thatcher?

Whatever the cause of Clydebank's decline at least one part of it deserves some praise. The Park Bar was a very welcome sight to us.

Dumbarton, the bit down by the river at least, was much better than we expected it to be. The two pubs we visited were quite good as well. So we have no complaints.

A few miles further up the road we found The Coach House Inn at Cardross. It is a well-equipped, slightly up market country pub. Probably a good place for Sunday lunches but not really up to much as a venue for wild stag parties.

Kilcreggan is one of our favourite places to stop for a quiet beer, or two if the notion takes us. We would certainly recommend it as a great wee place to stop for refreshment. Just don't mention our names. It might go against you.

This trip earned a combined score of 3 out of 5, placing it in 5th position on our list of trips. It has to be said that this is a hell of a lot higher than we would have predicted.

We Wiz Framed

(Two new stars of the silver screen?
Or two old has-beens, it's yet to be seen)

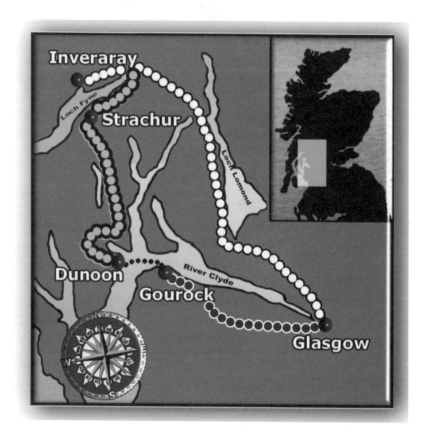

EK-Glasgow-Inveraray-Strachur-Dunoon
Gourock-Glasgow-EK
(Four Buses/Two Trains/One Ferry)

John; A couple of weeks before this trip, my youngest son Gregor said to me that he and his partner Michelle would like to come on a trip with us and record it with a view to producing a pod cast and putting it on U-tube (I think).

I thought he was kidding, but he wasn't. Gregor works in a film production company and has had his name on the telly a couple of times as the Editor of the program. The wife and I are really pleased. Michelle works in radio as a producer, and she is dead clever, so they both know what they are doing. I still thought they were crazy to think that our first book attempt was any good, but Michelle thinks it is great. Hope her taste in men is better.

Craig and I (especially Craig) were very nervous about trying to be humorous with the camera on us, so we had several meetings to work out what to say to make us spontaneously funny. We just ended up getting pissed and not thinking of anything funny.

So we planned a trip that we thought would be scenic. By that I mean missing out places like Greenock, Port Glasgow, Saltcoats etc. I could go on for ages.

Mind you, I was a bit worried that the places we were visiting would be a bit posh, which usually means there are no characters or drunks in the pubs at 11.00am to have a chat and a good laugh with.

I gave Gregor the details of the trip and said he could meet us in Glasgow, but he wanted to get the whole trip recorded. So at 7.30am, they arrived at our house so they could film Kate (the luckiest women in the world) having the honour of making my Corned Beef and English Mustard pieces (plain bread of course).

Kate was dead nervous and almost cut her hand off. I had to warn her to be careful not to waste the pieces.

So we were ready to leave at the appointed time of 7.50am and Kate waved us off, hoping to get on the film. She had spent hours making sure she looked great for the camera. She didn't need to worry, she always looks great. (what a crawler).

Craig: This trip almost planned itself. It all started when John announced at one of our frequent planning meetings in "The Lum" that we would be having company on our next trip. I actually thought that he meant another dedicated bevy merchant would be joining us.

When he explained who it was I have to admit I thought he was losing it. Why on earth would any young couple want to be seen with us never mind having to listen to our increasingly rambling nonsense all day?

The real reason they wanted to come turned out to be even weirder than I could have imagined. It did present us with a bit of a problem though. We needed to find an interesting route but not one we had already done. As it turned out we did do a trip, part of which we had done before. However, we made sure we visited different pubs this time around, and let's face it, that's all that really counts, isn't it?

John; We got to Craig and Irene's house to pick up Craig, and what a laugh. Normally Craig answers the door with his pieces in hand and off we go, but not when a camera is about. This is no kidding, Irene had spent days cleaning and tidying the house and was up early getting ready for our arrival. Women are something else. We were invited in to the living room which looked nothing like I had ever seen it, tidy.

So Irene said goodbye to Craig, it was like a scene out of "Gone with the Wind" or some other Chick Flick.

So we wandered down the few steps to the Murray Road, trying to be funny, and got on the No. 16 bus to take us right into Buchanan Street Bus Station.

Gregor's a great laugh and cannot be embarrassed. On the bus and everywhere else he would film us and anyone else that happened to be about. Some of the Jakies on the bus thought we must be snoopers for the Social Security. Gregor didn't care-what a boy.

We were held up in a traffic jam for a while and thought that we may miss the Inveraray bus at 9.30am, so we started thinking up different journeys if this happened, but all was ok as the last bit of the journey to the bus station went quickly-we got all the lights.

Craig; *Personally, I wasn't fazed by the idea of a film crew following us around, recording our innermost thoughts for posterity. John, on the other hand, was a bag of nerves. My one concession to the filming was replacing my usual crumpled plastic bag with a much more stylish rucksack. From the very start it seemed like we wouldn't manage the proposed route. The number 16 bus took ages travelling down to Glasgow. Not that I really noticed. I was far too busy being totally embarrassed by the filming going on around us. John's son, Gregor, filmed us from every conceivable angle, none of them too flattering, I would imagine. I found it very hard to make eye contact with any of the other passengers. What they made of all this nonsense doesn't bear thinking about. They didn't look too amused anyway. Then again it was 8.00am on a dreich Wednesday morning so, there was no real reason for anyone to be laughing their heads off.*

Against all the odds we made it in plenty of time for our next bus.

John; As the weather forecast for the day was miserable, we did not have the usual problem of dozens of old fogies racing to be first on the bus. Today it was only Craig barging his way to the front.

Although the weather was dull, it stayed dry for the journey to Inveraray. The scenery was great and we all enjoyed the trip and arrived at about 11.15am, missing the first 15 minutes of opening hours.

We had a walk along the front and up to the pier where the "Vital Spark" was moored in all her glory as the picture I took shows (if Craig decides to put my picture in).

With Gregor filming and Michelle recording our every word, we wandered up the main street, which is called "Main Street" and into *"The George"* which is the only proper bar in the town. It is a lovely bar with stone walls, wooden ceiling with all the original beams and a log fire. You would think that this would make it the perfect bar, but it isn't.

The problem is that Craig and I like an old man's type of bar, but this was a bar where the barman (who was from somewhere in Eastern Europe), didn't, or couldn't talk to us. This didn't fit the bill of our idea of a good bar. But it is a lovely looking place and the pints were ok, although Craig complained his lager wasn't cold enough. We are getting used to the prices nowadays in places like this, although £6.40 for two pints was a bit steep.

Two auld yins often seen steaming along the Clyde.

We Wiz Framed

I think it would be a good idea if pubs reduced their prices between 11.00am and 5.00pm for bus pass holders. We would like it anyway.

Our next bus did not leave till the back of two, so we managed about three pints and by the time we left, the place was packed with a funeral party, kids and a man wearing a kilt and an Aran Sweater. Talk about being glad to get out of a place!

The Barman did his best, but the funeral party was a bit too much for him.

Barman Rating; 🍺🍺

Craig; Being an old hand at long distance bus travel I knew that we had to be extremely vigilant about keeping our place in the queue. To the untrained eye everything looked quiet and peaceful. But that's what they want you to think. We had been caught out in similar circumstances before. This time I was taking no chances. I could see some of the oldies circling round for a pincer attack on the front of the queue. Grabbing John's arm I moved to the front and cut them off in their stride. Although to be honest, most of them were shuffling forward rather than striding.

I was still congratulating myself on out maneuvering them when I got on to the bus. The ticket scanner was, for some unexplained reason, sitting on the floor. I had to go back down a step in order to reach it. Even then I nearly landed on my head trying to place my card on it. Having seen the state of some of my fellow passengers, at least one was on crutches, this situation had the potential to become a bit of a horror story. I couldn't bear to watch them trying to use the machine. Since I didn't hear any screaming or snapping of brittle bones, I felt certain we had managed to get away without serious injury.

Usually the early stages of our journeys are fairly quiet and uneventful, not this one. Michelle, our sound recordist, had placed a microphone between the seats in front of us. The problem was we kept forgetting it was there. We really must demand editorial control over the content of that tape. I would estimate that it is probably 90% utter drivel, 6% libel and 3% likely to upset the easily offended. That means 1% of the recorded material might be usable. Whether or not it might be of any interest is anybody's guess.

We arrived at our first stop of the day, Inveraray, in reasonable weather. Not wishing to waste too much time in taking in the scenery, we made straight for the "George Hotel". Almost immediately I realized that I wasn't going to like the George. There was nothing really wrong with the hotel, it's just that it wasn't what I like in a pub. Quite probably there are thousands of tourists around the world who would sing the praises of this place. It had lots of authentic wood paneling, wooden benches, chairs and even exposed rafters. Actually the benches looked like old church pews. Perhaps if it had been a smaller bar area I would have liked it better. There was just too much wood for my liking.

I could be wrong but I got the impression that we were the only Scottish customers in the place. It seemed to me that the George makes most of its money from selling bar meals. We must have been a great disappointment to the owners. Once again it seemed to me that a perfectly good pub atmosphere was being sacrificed to pack in as many free spending tourists as possible.

John; We left ourselves enough time to wander down to the front street, which is called "Front Street" and visit the bar in "*The Argyll Hotel*". This had no atmosphere at all, although the people behind the bar were nice and the lady who ran the place gave me her address so I could send her a copy of our first book, "The Cheap Way Round" which I was talking about to anyone who would listen. She says she has dozens of relatives who would love it. So there you go. In the meantime, Gregor and Michelle were recording everything, and as the pints went down, Craig and I felt we were getting funnier. Aye, right.

Barmaid Rating;

After we finished our pints, we went into the "Front Street" and over to the bus stop. There was a bus up a bit from the stop and I didn't realize it was for us. Suddenly the doors opened, two locals jumped on and we only just realized it was our bus and got on before it left. You would think the driver would have backed up and let us know what was happening. Bus drivers are something else.

The Creggans Inn, a wee bit on the quiet side, apart from father /son sporting grudge matches.

It was a lovely run round to Strachur, our next port of call, and we were hoping the pubs would be a bit more entertaining. We got off at the first, which was *"The Creggans Inn"*. This was a wee bit outside the town, but since there was only one other pub in the town, we thought we would give this one a try.

There was nothing wrong with the bar. It was nice and had a pool room and dart board. The problem again was there was no one else in the place and the barmaid disappeared after serving us. Because there were four of us we had a great time, as we did all day (and night). The bar had a great wee dog which attached itself to Gregor and Michelle and was great fun. Wish people were as much fun as dogs and try to mount you all the time, well the ladies anyway.

Gregor and I had a couple of games of Pool and then we tried to say goodbye to the barmaid who had disappeared.

Barmaid Rating; 🍺 (does nobody in Scotlands' tourist industry even try)

Craig; John was complaining that bars were not as good as they used to be. This is a favourite topic of John's; in fact it crops up on every trip. He claims that in the old days even if you went into a pub on your own you could always chat away with the barman. I told him that if he wanted a chinwag with this barman he had better brush up on his Polish language skills.

The weather was beginning to deteriorate by the time we left the George. This gave us the perfect excuse to once again ignore the scenic grandeur of Inveraray and make straight for the "Argyle Hotel". The lounge of the hotel is very well upholstered, lots of comfy looking couches and chairs. Michelle probably saved me from a terrible fate when she stopped me from sitting down on one of the comfiest looking couches. It was so soft and welcoming that I could well have disappeared into it. I have enough trouble getting out of low chairs without being swallowed by one of those overstuffed blancmanges.

Once, in a hotel in Port William, I sat down in a similar couch to have a bar meal. I sank down so low that I nearly slapped my chin on the edge of the table. There then followed a full two minute pantomime as I struggled to get up out of the bloody thing. At least it seemed to entertain my fellow diners.

Anyway, back in the Argyle Hotel John was doing his salesman bit with anyone who would listen to him. Strange to tell but he did seem to be drumming up a bit of interest. John is convinced that our first book will sell well given the reaction to it from the people we meet. It will be interesting to see if his tactic of giving away free copies of the book will ever result in a sale. You just never know.

I must say it did help our credibility a bit having Gregor and Michelle shadowing us.

We left the hotel with only minutes to spare before our next bus was due to leave for Strachur. I will spare some blushes by not mentioning the near arsing up of our entire day by a certain bus planner. The weather was closing in a bit by now but we still decided to stop at "The Creggans Hotel". Looking back on it that was probably a mistake. Not that the hotel was too bad, it was quite good actually, but it stopped us from getting to "The Clachan" dry. It would also have saved me from having to listen to John whining about the "forced march" through torrential rain.

The Creggans Hotel was clean and tidy with a decent pint of lager on sale. That being said, we all agreed that there was something lacking in the atmosphere of the place. It therefore struck me as a little bit strange that the Creggan's turned out to be a two pint stop. Could it have anything to do with a bit of father/son rivalry on the pool table? Fortunately for all of us the honours were even. It wouldn't do to upset the cameraman. They say the camera never lies, but in the wrong hands it could definitely start a few nasty rumours.

John; We all went out to what Craig said was a short walk to the next pub. Short walk my arse, and it was pouring. By the time we got to the pub in the village, *"The Clachan"*, we were soaked and as I walked up the road in the rain I was fantasizing about a lovely warm wee pub with a roaring fire, friendly barman and a couple of lively locals. You wouldn't believe it, but that's exactly what it was.

"The Clachan" is a fantastic bar with a great barman and the three or four locals who were in were great fun and made us really welcome. It was one of the best bars I have visited and we had some great laughs.

You know how in a bar after a few pints men start talking a load of rubbish, well at one stage we were all talking about the ratio of straight men to gay men. The barman assured us that one in seven men was gay. There were six men in the bar at this stage and we all assured each other we were not gay, not that's there's anything wrong at all with being gay.

That's the new John talking. Just then the door opened and a guy walked in, so we all started singing 'you're a poof' to him.

John's patter was so entertaining that this bloke actually slipped into a coma.

The old John returns. He just turned round and showed us his arse. What a laugh.

The time till our next bus just flew in. I was really pleased for Gregor and Michelle that we had found a really great pub and had such a good time in it. We were sorry to leave and promised to return as soon as possible, which we will. The barman even bought us a round even though he knew we were leaving shortly, what a guy. He even knew East Kilbride and one of his regulars used to be a neighbour of ours when he was a boy and now has one of his houses in the village and must be a millionaire, at least, and a great guy as well.

So with a heavy heart and choruses of "We'll meet again" filling the air, we boarded our bus to Dunoon.

Barman Rating; 🍺🍺🍺🍺🍺

Gregor thinks the signs are looking good.

We Wiz Framed

Craig; I have to admit that the distance between the Creggans and the Clachan was perhaps a bit longer than I had made out to John. There is a perfectly good reason for this but my travelling companion was in no mood to listen to it. Quite simply the reason for the discrepancy was that I had never actually travelled along that road. I had looked at the area on 'Google Earth' and just guessed the distance. I guessed badly. The hard slog to the Clachan was worth it. What a great wee pub. This could quite possibly be the best pub we have visited so far on our travels.

It should be remembered of course that I was quite possibly suffering from exhaustion and advanced hypothermia by the time we got there. Once we had defrosted, John swung back into salesman mode and started telling the patrons all about our book. They seemed to like the idea, in fact the owner was so taken with the idea he bought us all a drink. That was a first for us. We may well have done a little victory dance.

With all the laughing and joking, not to mention the drinking, I think maybe we all forgot about the fact that Michelle was still taping everything. The conversation became less than PC. One of the guys in the bar declared that he'd read that one in eight people are gay. Someone else then shouted out that if that was true the next person to come into the bar must be the gay of the village. There were seven of us already inside. As if on cue, an unwary poor soul stepped through the door to wild applause and a few jocular and crude comments. He took it well, considering. All too soon it was time to go. So it was handshakes all round, another first, and off we went back out into the rain. I think we all knew that after the 'Clachan' everything else was likely to be a bit of an anti-climax.

John; Although it was still wet and dull, we enjoyed the journey, and I think I finished my pieces on the bus. They were great.

We visited two pubs in the town, *"Mac Clures Bar" and "The Ingram Bar"*. We had a pint in both of them and they were nice enough bars, but after *"The Clachan"* the next bars were on a hiding to nothing.

Barmen Ratings for two pubs;

For those of you who have never visited Dunoon, it is a great we toon, but every time you stand up you'll want to sit doon.

The time for the departure of the ferry was fast approaching, so I left a minute or so before Craig and the kids and hurried down to the pier and got the tickets, just as well.

Michelle proving she knows a lot about sound but not much about pictures as she walks into my photo of the pub

By the time Craig and the kids got to the gangway, the guy waiting to cast off was in a state and was not happy, even though he could see Craig was struggling to get any speed up, what with the wind blowing and his arthritis, it was a miracle he could move as fast as he did. They made it with a minute to spare before the departure time, but the wee man was still in a bad mood. I won't go on any more about my opinion of many of the people in this country who deal with the public. Let's just tiptoe round the issue and say that some of them are arseholes.

We had a lovely sail over to Gourock, even in wild conditions. A wee swally as we sailed over helped greatly.

Craig; We have been to Dunoon on a few occasions during our travels. Usually we have a pint or two in the pub nearest the ferry terminal, called "The View". This time we planned to visit two other pubs. It's a pity they weren't very busy as you never really see a pub at its best when they're empty.

"Mac Clures Bar" is quite an old fashioned pub, but I liked it a bit. Although the pub looks really small from the outside it has quite a long bar with a high ceiling. We were spoilt for choice as far as finding a seat was concerned since there were very few customers at that time of day. The lack of atmosphere meant we didn't stay long. Just up the road we had a pint in "The Ingram". It has a bright little bar and is quite a comfortable place to spend a little time. Once again we found that this bar was very quiet.

Down at the pier I very nearly missed the ferry. The wee man at the gang plank looked ready to have a stroke by the time I managed to reach the boat. It's not as if the tide was turning or anything else of a nautical nature was likely to go wrong. The boat was nearly empty. You'd think they would be pleased to have the custom.

Just to calm my shattered nerves we had a wee drink on the boat.

John; Our train to Glasgow was leaving a few minutes after we got off the ferry, and as it was a long walk up and down two platforms that were built when trains must have been a mile long, we had to rush. We just made it and Craig was really knackered by the time he got on. It's hard to believe this, but the guard tried to close the doors when Craig was about three feet from stepping onto the train. I managed to block the doors and luckily Craig got on safely, but what is that all about? Calling the guard an arsehole is unfair. An arsehole is a useful thing.

I wonder if any tourist comes to Scotland more than once, I doubt it if they have to deal with people who work for any branch of our transport system.

The journey into Glasgow Central was uneventful and after getting off the train (I'm not sure how to spell alighting), we wandered round to our regular Glasgow haunt, *"The Horshoe Bar"* and had an enjoyable pint in a great atmosphere before wandering back to the station and getting the train to EK. I have no idea what time it was, but it was dark, I think.

To be honest (and drunk) I don't remember too much about the journey back to EK, although I remember wandering through the village into *"The Monty"* for our regular end to the evening. I remember meeting an old friend whom I had not seen for a long while, so I couldn't have been too bad.

Kate came down in the car, picked us up and took us all home. So ended another great day out.

Having Gregor and Michelle with us, although a bit nerve racking at first, made the day even better and Craig and I are looking forward to seeing their results. To be honest, we both are a bit worried as we think we were not at our best, aye right.

Craig; On the train back to Glasgow I once again reminded Gregor and Michelle of our agreement about not recording sleeping drunks on trains. As far as I can tell they kept their word. I suppose only time and a wary eye on u-tube will tell about that.

Not wishing to defy tradition we visited "The Horseshoe" as soon as we arrived in Glasgow. John was very much on a roll today and once again started talking up our book to anyone who would listen. Apart from that I don't really remember much of what happened in The Horseshoe.

"The Monty" was our last port of call of the evening, once again in keeping with tradition. Apparently we had quite a good time in there. John's wife Kate collected us from the pub once again. Usually that would be the end of my evening. Unfortunately I had made a very bad miscalculation early on in the day. I had forgotten that Irene would not be at home till after midnight. My mistake was to leave my key behind when I left the house in the morning.

The upshot was that I had to phone a taxi to take me to where Irene was babysitting. Checking my pockets the next morning I came to the conclusion that I had given the driver a tip larger than the actual fare. It's just a pity the concession card doesn't work in taxis.

That's the problem wi' filming us drinking pints; too many retakes.

In Summary

Everybody knows that Inveraray is a tourist hot spot. And if you like to do a bit of sightseeing, it's a great place to do it. But if a comfy wee pub to relax in is more your idea of fun, you might want to try somewhere else. That somewhere else could be The Clachan Bar in the village of Strachur. Should you find yourself in the Cowal area a wee visit to the Clachan is highly recommended. We had ourselves a great time in there.

Down in Dunoon there is a good selection of pubs to choose from, apparently there is some scenery there as well.

When we were there the pubs were a bit on the quiet side, but mid-week, most pubs are nowadays.

Today's journey scored a disappointing 2.5. Meaning it came in at number eleven on the list. It was very much a case of all of the rest of the pubs dragging down the top scoring Clachan Bar.

Given our experience, it might be a good idea to get down to the pier with plenty of time to spare for the ferry over to Gourock.

It would appear that collecting tickets is a highly stressful job as the guys who do it seem to be a very excitable group of people. This is true for both the ferry and the train. So to avoid all that frothing at the mouth or even a potential stroke, give these wee blokes a break and arrive that extra five minutes early.

Bordering on a Dry Run

(To have a good bevy is our stated mission
But doon in Creetown they've got prohibition)

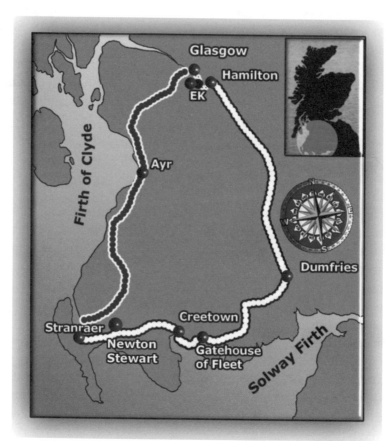

*East Kilbride-Hamilton-Dumfries
Gatehouse of Fleet-Creetown
Newton Stewart-Stranraer-EK*
(Six Buses Three Trains)

Bordering on a Dry Run

John; Craig organized this trip, including which pubs we were visiting. This included going into Google Maps to check up on all the pubs. I want to make this clear right from the start so you will know who to blame for the balls-ups that followed.

It was a glorious day, the first for ages, as I wandered down to pick up Craig at 8.20am. Craig's wife Irene was not all done up as there was no film crew following us today (there was the last time).

We got the 201 bus to Hamilton. The only thing of interest on the journey was at EK bus station when Craig said something to me, I thought he said "hat", but it was the word "that" he had said, hearing getting worse. However I looked up and a Jakie was getting on the bus with a pink skip cap covered in silver sparkly things, it looked ridiculous, even by Jakie standards in EK. He caused no trouble on the bus, just the usual talking to people through his one nostril and saying 'hingmie' all the time.

At Hamilton Bus Station there were dozens of the Silver Headed waiting at our bus stance and we were a bit worried about getting a seat. However they were all waiting for a couple of Caledonian Tour buses. It's a laugh watching them all trying to be first on the bus to get the best seat. I'm sure the ones who get the front seats are treated like lepers for the rest of the journey.

Our bus, the Stagecoach X74 (good bus information eh!) arrived and we got seated and enjoyed our run down to Dumfries. On the journey the bus stopped at Moffat. This looks like a nice wee place, if not a bit English looking. I took a photo out of the bus window of a statue of a big ram. Don't know why it's there or why I took the photo, but it looked nice.

Craig; This trip was set to be one of the longest journeys we had ever made. It was quite complicated to plan but I thought I was up to the task. We were heading down to one of my favourite parts of the country; Galloway. Many years ago I used to do quite a lot of hillwalking and canoeing in the area, so I felt well qualified to be in charge of all the arrangements for our day's travelling.

Things don't always turn out the way you plan them. That's a phrase I should have tattooed on my arm. I would imagine that after this effort John might prefer it if I had it chiselled into my forehead. In my defence I would like to say that some things just cannot be predicted.

Even before we started out I tried to explain to John that there were certain aspects of this trip which could be problematic. But as usual he wasn't listening. Anyway, when we decided to make the trip to Galloway I made up my mind to do my very best to create a flawless schedule.

My trusty computer coughed out all the details. I then used 'Google Earth' to check out the availability of any well-appointed refreshment stops in our proposed destinations. Everything checked out. Just to put John's nose out of joint I produced a full colour spread sheet showing all our arrival and departure times. It was a minor work of art, if I do have to say so myself, and I do. The D-Day landings had less planning than our little excursion.

John; The sun was shining when we got off the bus at the bus station in Dumfries. After checking what stance our next bus left from, we wandered over to Craig's first choice of pub. It was called *"World's End"*. A great name and gives the impression of an old dingy place with smoke stained walls etc. Bugger me if the owners hadn't spent a fortune doing the place up. It was like walking into some spotless place, all white walls and slate tiled floors. Don't get me wrong, it was very nice and the barmaid, Margaret, who was the owner, was great. She spent some time reading our last book in which we slagged off another pub in Dumfries. She agreed with all we said. Mind you she would, wouldn't she?

At that time, 11.15am on a Monday, the place was very quiet, although a regular came in and asked us where we came from. Problem was he was as deaf as a post, so that conversation finished up quickly enough. He kept speaking to Margaret who was great, and very patient with him. What a great wee bloke. We said our goodbyes to Margaret, and shouted them to the wee deaf bloke and headed out into the sunshine to find Craig's next pub.

Barmaid Rating; ▓▓▓▓ (great at dealing with the hard of hearing and old farts like us)

Craig; I had looked at quite a few pubs in Dumfries as we had about an hour and three quarters to kill. It struck me that it would be a good idea to keep to an area quite close to the bus station. This would stop us from getting lost and, more importantly, we wouldn't be wasting any of our precious time wandering around the streets.

My first choice of pub was the 'World's End', and what an excellent choice it was.

John got really excited when he caught a whiff of bleach as we entered the place. He is a very strange man! I have to admit the pub was absolutely spotless. We don't often get to say that about the pubs we visit. The owners were both very welcoming and we chatted away to them for a while.

Unfortunately, since it was only just after eleven o'clock, the place was empty. Things brightened up a bit when a wee man came in and began talking to us. It got a bit surreal to be honest as it turned out that he was profoundly deaf. I'm fairly sure he knew he was deaf, so I couldn't help but wonder why he would want to get into a question and answer session with two complete strangers. John was shouting at the top of his voice but the old guy just wasn't getting it. I pretended to study my mobile phone so that he wouldn't involve me in his one sided conversation.

After finishing our pints we made our way along to our second pub of the day; 'The White Hart'. I was justifying my choice of this pub to John as we walked along the road. 'The White Hart' is a famous name in pub terms. It's a name with great historical significance; years ago many towns throughout Britain would have had an inn of that name. My historical ravings were suddenly cut short. It was shut. We moved on. To be honest I don't think we missed very much.

Where shutting time really is the end of the world

Walking back the way we had come we passed the 'Old Abbot's Vaults'. John suggested we nip in for a quick beer. I had to remind him that in our first book we had slagged off the place, not to mention its customers, to such a degree we might well be lucky to get away with a severe arse kicking if we ever went back in. John's cowardice kicked in and we slunk past 'The Vaults' on the other side of the road.

We made our way to English Street as I'd remembered seeing a couple of pubs there on my computer. 'Dickie's Bar' wasn't quite what I was expecting. On my computer screen it looked a bit seedy and run down, in other words, our perfect pub. It still looked a bit ragged on the outside but inside it obviously has had a make-over. It was very neat and tidy. In fact I'm almost sure I could smell just the hint of bleach in the air.

The beer was good and the wee barman was fairly pleasant, but something was missing. After a swift pint, so were we.

John; The next pub Craig had chosen was *"The White Hart"*, it was shut, so we walked up a nice wee lane passed a couple of nice looking wee pubs until we eventually found his next pub, *"Dickies Bar"*, Craig said he liked the name (remember he's from Auchinleck, so I give him a bit of leeway).

There was nothing wrong with the pub and the guy behind the bar was pleasant enough, but there was nothing of note about it. For me it was a bit too modern in its décor. So after giving Craig a minor slagging we left for our next adventure, worrying if it would be open.

Barman Rating; 🍺🍺

We wandered back down the way we had come and into *"The Victoria Inn"*. There was only about 15 minutes till our next bus, so we had a half pint. I was bursting for the toilet so Craig had to order the half pints. He's never ordered half pints in his life and was amazed at what they looked like. This was a nice enough pub, but the barmaid was not very talkative. However with only about 10 minutes to finish our "halves" and walk to the bus station, her silence didn't matter.

Barmaid Rating; 🍺🍺 (is a friendly word too much to ask for).

We waited in the sunshine and ate some of our pieces (regulars will be glad to note I'm still with the Corned Beef with English Mustard on Plain Bread).

Craig; John started getting a bit twitchy about catching our next bus. Actually it might have had more to do with his bladder obsession. He knew we had an hour long bus journey ahead of us, along a winding, bumpy road. That is a nightmare scenario for older beer drinking men.

I somehow managed to convince him that we should visit one more pub before we left Dumfries. We would have missed a little gem if we'd passed up a chance to visit the Victoria Inn. As we stepped into the bar we also stepped back into the early 1970s. With the exception of a couple of flat screen televisions I doubt if anything had changed in this pub in several decades. All the pictures on the walls had faded into sepia tones, which seemed to match some of the clientele. Or maybe that was just a trick of the light.

Time and John's capacity to retain liquids meant that we had to limit ourselves to half pints. John, in an effort to resolve one of these problems, made a beeline for the toilets, leaving me to order the drinks. He knows I hate ordering half pints. I couldn't believe the price the barmaid demanded for the two test tubes of beer she put on the bar. The one good thing about it was that we were able to drink them in seconds.

We made our way down to the bus station to wait for our bus to Gatehouse of Fleet. It was really sunny by this time and I was looking forward to the journey.

John; Our next bus, a Stagecoach 500 arrived and on we got. By the way, the reason I know all the bus numbers is that Craig produced a detailed spread sheet with all this information. Pity he hadn't checked the pub opening hours that closely, but more of that later.

Our next port of call was Gatehouse of Fleet. For some reason I always thought it was next to Blackpool. The sun was still shining and the place looked lovely, but not a place I thought would have good men's pubs. So we wandered into *"The Masonic Arms"*, it was all low wooden ceilings, carpets and brass fittings etc. Nothing wrong with this if you're out with the wife, but certainly not a pub for a laugh. So we went out into the beer garden, which worryingly enough, had kids' toys all over the place.

We finished our pints. I'm sure the barman checks the fingerprints to make sure your holding the glass in the correct Masonic manner, if not you don't get in again. I doubt we'll be returning.

Barman Rating;  (didn't speak to him long enough to give him any less).

The Ship Inn is number one on my list of pubs never to be visited again. (It's a long list by the way)

Craig, with his belief in Google still to the fore, said there was a great pub at the end of the road called *"The Ship Inn"*. We wandered down this up-markety sort of town till we reached the Ship and in I wandered, leading the way. It was about ten past two by the way.

The sign outside had four stars on it, we had no idea what this meant, but we agreed it was impressive.

The bar was like something in an up-market airport, if you know what I mean, which you probably don't. The girl behind the bar put on an artificial smile and asked what we wanted. I said, using my best Govan, a pint of Lager and a pint of Best. You could have knocked me down with a feather when she replied, 'we can't sell alcohol after 2.00pm because of the licensing laws'. What the hell was she talking about? I had no idea. The best reply I could come up with was 'you're kidding'. She wasn't.

This is a four star place in a tourist area which is, I would imagine, looking for business. Honest, only in Scotland. The wife and I were in Tenerife recently where you could get a pint in dozens of places for one euro, and they were open all day, and night. The tourist industry in this country is crap. Thank god we're not tourists.

Barmaid Rating ⊔ (stuck-up barmaid should be ashamed of herself).

Craig; When we were passing through Castle Douglas I felt a little sorry that I hadn't managed to schedule a wee refreshment stop there as it has some really nice bars on the main street which I have sampled a few times. The reason I hadn't included them this time was quite simple, to me at least. It occurred to me that visiting pubs in smaller towns would give us a better feeling for the area than visiting the more touristy pubs in a big market town like Castle Douglas.

I suppose you could say that I was looking for the quirkier side of country life. We certainly got that, and then some.

While planning this trip to Gatehouse of Fleet I pulled out all the stops. I searched every inch of the place on the internet. It really is a great system. As soon as the bus entered the town I knew exactly where everything was.

Bordering on a Dry Run

We decided to visit the Masonic Arms which is located at the eastern end of the town, just off the main street. John suggested that maybe they were trying to keep it a secret. We resisted the urge to take daft pictures outside the front door of the pub. The public bar was almost empty so we took our beers outside to the beer garden. It is quite a big area with a few picnic style tables. We had to take shelter from the sun under a brolly, which is not something that happens very often on our travels. My pint was more than passable and we could quite easily have stayed for another but, as John pointed out, we were not there to enjoy ourselves. There were pubs out there which needed our attention.

I had been looking forward to visiting the pub at the other end of Gatehouse of Fleet. The Ship Inn certainly looked the part of a well maintained country pub. There is a sign on the side of the building which proudly states that it has been a hostelry since 1794.

You would think they would be good at it by now. But you'd be wrong. As a self-taught expert in all things relating to the licenced trade I was shocked at our treatment in this pub. Actually, once inside the place it didn't look very much like a country pub at all, more of a trendy lounge bar in the city.

That was bad enough, but to be refused a drink at two o'clock in the afternoon was unbelievable. The wee lassie behind the counter, I can't bring myself to call it a bar, asked us if she could help us. What she was prepared to help us with was never specified. We cheerily asked for a couple of beers. That's when I noticed the strange expression on her face. I thought she maybe couldn't understand our accents or perhaps wasn't used to people saying please. Still smiling, she said she couldn't sell us a drink because the place was only licenced up to 2pm. In my long and mostly distinguished career as a beer connoisseur I have never heard of such a ridiculous restriction on a licence. Even back in the bad old days of the 1970s the harshest limit saw afternoon closing set at 2.30pm.

Maybe we were refused service because we ordered beer and not something more exotic like afternoon cocktails, if there is such a thing. After spending a fortune turning their couthy wee pub into a posh posing palace maybe the owners have become a bit picky about who they allow into their premises. To be honest, it wouldn't be the first time we had brought the tone of some place down just by being in it. To say I was seething just didn't cover it. I was verging on the homicidal!

John; After that shock we wandered back up the main road a bit. Craig was quiet, I knew he felt humiliated. I was having a great time. We went into a pub, or hotel, I'm not sure, called, I think *"The Nook of Fleet"*. Again, there was nothing wrong, but nothing right about it. We ended up in a beer garden, again. At least the sun was shining and the beer was good. I think Craig was cheering up. This place was definitely nothing like Blackpool, where I'd rather have been.

Barman Rating; 🍺🍺 (didn't talk to him enough to give him a one).

Leaving a sunny Gatehouse of Fleet behind, we got on the Stagecoach X75 and had another lovely run through Galloway till we reached Creetown. This is a really lovely area, even if they try their best to make you feel unwelcome.

Again, Craig was confident. He had again checked out the pubs on Google!

Craig; We shipped out of the Ship Inn and made our way back up the street to the 'Bank of Fleet Hotel'. It was quite a good place to stop for a beer, especially an unexpected one. The bar area was spookily familiar. It was kitted out much like the no-go area that is the 'Ship Inn', all white pine and hard wood floors. Once again we sat out in the beer garden. This gave me a chance to calm down a bit, although, if I'd known what we

*were about to get ourselves into I think our day trip would have
ended right there.*

*Our bus to Creetown was dead on time and I felt confident all
our troubles were behind us. I had 'cased out' the entire town
via the net and all the main points of interest, the pubs to be
precise, had been noted and their locations committed to
memory. Everything was perfect, or so we thought.*

*Creetown looked like a nice two pub stop for two thirsty
travellers. We had to stay thirsty for a bit longer than I had
planned for.*

**The Ellangowan Hotel. An impressive building, but we
we're less than impressed with its opening hours.**

John; Getting off the bus on the main street, which was the
only street, we wandered back along the road to the first of the
two pubs we would visit. This one was called *"The Barholm*

Arms". It was shut. So, with Craig's confidence on the ebb, and my slagging in full flow, we wandered back up to the other end of the street to the next pub, which was also a hotel. It was called *"The Ellangowan Hotel"*. It was shut. This was no longer funny. We had about an hour and a half stuck in this dry town. Even I felt sorry for Craig, but only for a moment.

Being observant and desperate, I had noticed there was a beer garden behind this hotel (Galloway is famous for closed pubs and beer gardens) and along the road was a general store and offie (wee shop that sells bevy).

So we headed along the only road in the town towards the wee shop. On the way along the road, we noticed a wee ice cream shop, I love ice cream, and the older I get, the more I like it,- wonder why. We went in and at once Craig, who is very clean by nature, decided he didn't want anything. I had a cone from a wee man who licked his fingers before picking up the cone. Now I'm not very fussy about hygiene, but for Christ sake what's that all about? The ice cream was soft, but shouldn't have been. Fifty pence down the drain and the cone in the first bin we came to. At least the place was open.

We found the general store which was open and were relieved to see it sold bevy, so we bought four cans of lager and wandered back up and into the beer garden at the back of the shut hotel. Craig was sure we were breaking some law. I agreed that it was the one about enjoying yourself on a day out in Scotland. I must admit it was very nice sitting in the sunshine enjoying our cans.

Just as we were about to finish, a wee man who looked as if he knew where he was going came round through the beer garden. After some pleasantries and trying to find out how many bye laws we were breaking, I asked him if he was going to open the hotel bar, he said yes, but at five o'clock. So into the hotel he went and left us to our own devices. I'm sure that in any other country where tourists are welcome, a person in his position would have invited us in and poured us a pint, but there you go.

Bar persons Rating; What f'n bar persons

Our visit to Creetown ended with us waiting about 40 minutes for a bus as the one Craig had planned to get didn't turn up. During the time we were waiting Craig, who was in a bad mood, had a run in with the village idiot who stopped as he was cycling by to ask us what we were waiting for. I can't even begin to put in print Craig's reply. Needless to say the village idiot buggered off sharply. Having slagged the idiot off there was nothing else to do but hang about the bus stop complaining about rural bus services.

I didn't want to mention, but did, that almost everything that day had been a screw up. Eventually Craig said something along the lines that if I was so f****** smart I could organize trips from now on. I think I managed to placate him by saying that it was not his fault and that the day's problems could have happened to anyone. I didn't mention anyone from Auchinleck.

'Am telling ye it's definitely shut!

Bordering on a Dry Run

Craig; *We got off the bus in the centre of the town and walked back towards the first of our intended venues, 'The Barholm Arms' I had caught a glimpse of it as we had passed in the bus and I was a worried man. There wasn't much sign of life. I was clinging on to the hope that my imagination was working overtime. As there were no nicotine addicts hanging around the front door of the pub I took that as a sure sign that it was shut. I was correct.*

At this point I couldn't look John in the eye. He was obviously crushed by this set back, I know I was. You could have cut the silence with a broken beer glass on the long trudge back along the street. The omens were not good. We hadn't seen a living soul since we got off the bus and the street in front of us was still completely empty. I fully expected to see a tumble weed rolling down the pavement.

I had been looking forward to supping a beer or two in 'The Ellangowan Hotel'. The hotel is quite famous among horror film fans as it was featured in the cult classic 'The Wicker Man' back in the 70's. It turned out that it was about to feature in another horror. This one featured John and me, and we didn't like the script. The hotel was also closed, and looked like it had been for some time. John was speechless with frustration. Once again I couldn't look at him directly but I'm sure I caught a glimpse of a small tear rolling down his cheek. Actually he wasn't completely speechless. He did manage to utter a few words, they didn't form sentences, but they were quite descriptive, not to say hurtful.

We just stood there for a while, after all there didn't seem to be much else to do. To fill in the time John decided to find a toilet. It's what he does in times of stress.

After a few minutes we came up with a plan. John had spotted an off licence as we wandered up and down the street. Minutes later we were talking to the very pleasant young woman who was serving in the 'offie'. She told us that both the town's pubs

were still in operation but didn't open until 5pm. That would be half an hour after we were due to leave Creetown.
We drank our lukewarm lager in the deserted beer garden behind the hotel. It wasn't great but it was better than nothing, by a very small margin. This was not how I saw things panning out when I put in all those hours on my computer. Just to top off a wonderful visit our bus out of the dammed place didn't turn up. A lesser man would have been contemplating suicide by this time. There was nothing else for it but to hang about the bus stop practising our swearing. At one point the village idiot decided to give us the benefit of his wit. He shouted to us that we shouldn't worry; the bus would definitely turn up, but maybe not today. He was lucky I was carrying a bus pass and not a baseball bat. To lighten the moment I said to John that this joker could be described as the Creetown Cretin. Neither of us laughed.

John contains his enthusiasm for Creetown.

John; We eventually got on the bus, not the 431, but another bus. I was so excited to get out of this desolate place that I didn't notice the number. Craig, completely brassed off by now, said we were going to go straight to Stranraer and miss out Newton Stewart, but I managed to change his mind as we found out that the bus we got on stopped there. So although we got free tickets to Stranraer, we got off at Newton Stewart. You wouldn't do that if you were paying for your tickets. It's great to be old.

Newton Stewart is a great town, at least we thought so. So we wandered into the first pub we came to, called *"The Central Bar"*. This was more like the pubs we like, an old place with old guys in it.

As a wee aside to today's journey, a very interesting thing is that my pal Robin, who lives in Rothesay and has owned pubs there for over 30 years, had a spell of a few years running a pub in Newton Stewart, so I wondered if I could find anyone who had heard of him. I asked the barman, who said he had only been here for about four years, but the guy at the end of the bar, John McGregor, had worked in pubs in Newton Stewart all his life. So we called him over.

Low and behold (not allowed to say f*** me) he knew Robin well. He said that after he left Newton Stewart for Rothesay, about 50 or so regulars used to organize a weekend there about twice a year. He said that only about ten or so came back. Robin used to pipe them off the ferry and they'd all march up into Robin's pub 'The Glue Pot', and stay there for the weekend. Sounds crazy, but I've had weekends like that in Rothesay. So I was all chuffed to find out how popular Robin was. Wonder why he left Newton Stewart in such a hurry?

Barman Rating; ████

Craig; At exactly 5 o'clock, or opening time if you're from Creetown, our bus came roaring round the corner. By this time I was in what might be described as a foul mood and insisted

102

we should by-pass Newton Stewart and go straight on to Stranraer. Thankfully, John calmed me down and convinced me it would be better to stick to our schedule. I'm not sure if that was because he wanted a pint as soon as possible or, if he just wanted to give me yet another chance to embarrass myself even more with my dodgy planning.

Newton Stewart is a fairly big town. I have been visiting the place for many years now but John had never been there before. After a quick look around just to make sure there was an open pub or two in the place we made our way to the Central Bar. It was a good, traditional man's pub and it was quite busy. I was just glad it was open. The barman and the customers were friendly, the beer was both good and cold, and we enjoyed our short stay.

John; After an enjoyable drink and chat we wandered up to the bus station to find out when and where our bus left from. Craig insisted that I looked at the timetable on the bus stop so I could not blame him for another screw up.

We had about an hour to kill and were a bit hungry, especially Craig. Getting slagged all day must help the appetite. There was a carry out place just across the road called *"Star Fish Kebab"*. It was one of these places that sold everything. So in the spirit of adventure I had a bag of chips and Craig had a single fish. We sat in the sunshine and scoffed them. They were no bad.

Then we wandered across the other road and into *"The Star Inn"*. Robin's old pal John was in there as well and shouted over to us. We felt like real regulars. It was another great wee pub in the traditional way. Newton Stewart is a more traditional place in the pub sense. We were starting to enjoy ourselves. The drink was kicking in.

Although we were having a great time, we are slaves to the timetable and had to leave and head over to the bus station. All the locals in the bar shouted goodbye and told us to give Robin their best. We felt full of emulsion as we left the pub.

Barman Rating; ████

Craig; When we left the bar we made our way up the street, on the lookout for a chip shop. What we found was one of those three in one joints. It was part chip shop, part kebab shop and part pizza place. I've yet to get a decent meal out of one of these places and nothing changed that state of affairs on our visit to this one.

John didn't feel like risking his fragile health so opted for a bag of chips. I threw caution to the wind and ordered a single fish. You would think that with my track record that day I would've played it safe and gone for the chips as well. My fish was so hot I should have been wearing welding gloves to handle it. It had probably been lurking at the bottom of the fryer for a week or two.

After scorching my finger prints off not to mention cauterising my taste buds we ambled over to the Star Inn to cool down. This was another good little bar with an excellent pint of lager on offer. Once again the staff seemed friendly. I was so taken with the place that I had another half pint while John was using the facilities.

John; The bus station, which was just a bus stop, was bathed in sunshine, and we enjoyed the short wait for our next bus. The bus was a King of Kirkcowan's number 430, what a great name for a bus.

It set off and travelled at a hell of a rate. It would go off the main road and shoot through wee towns at about 70 miles an hour. God only knows what would happen if some kid wandered across the road when a bus was passing, maybe they know the timetables. Come to think about it, all the buses did this. It was scary. I told Craig I reckoned the drivers are desperate to get home before all the pubs close. That got no laugh from Craig. The pain of failure runs deep.

Bordering on a Dry Run

The problem we now had to face was that this was about half past six, the bus arrived in Stranraer about seven twenty and the train left at seven forty five, getting into Glasgow just after ten. This meant that we would get into Glasgow after about three and a half hours without a pint-and sober. This had never happened before, and wouldn't happen tonight.

Six cans of lager out of a Tesco Express in Stranraer we reckoned would do the trick. So after buying them, and some crisps, we wandered up to the train station. This is no easy feat in this depressing town. There are virtually no signs for the station which is positioned very handily if you are coming off a ferry, but a nightmare of a walk if you're not. But since the only reason for the town is because of the ferry to Ireland, it is understandable, except for grumpy old men like us.

It goes without saying, so I'll say it anyway, that since having a couple of cans on the train is an enjoyable experience, it is against one of the many crazy laws that this mad government has introduced to stop normal people enjoyable themselves. They bow down to the crazies and politically correct all the time.

Craig; The train from Stranraer left bang on time. It was almost empty. You have to ask yourself how viable this service is. We enjoyed our canned beer on the leisurely trip up to Ayr and then on to Glasgow on the second train.

It was too late to stop off in Glasgow for a quick brew so we caught the next train up to East Kilbride where Irene was waiting patiently to drive us home.

We had completed every part of our planned trip but we could hardly claim it as one of our most successful.

Personally I think it says an awful lot about the state of Scotland's tourist trade. What with pubs refusing to actually sell beer to thirsty customers, while others apparently design their opening hours to suit their staff it's little wonder people, especially the older variety, get a teeny bit peeved. Then, to top

things off, we have bus companies who seem to prefer a random approach to timetabling.
I think that in future I'll leave all of the planning for our journeys to John. Not just because he is better at it than me, and to be honest, who isn't? but for reasons of personal well-being. I was getting so wound up by all of the nonsense thrown up by this trip that at times I'm certain the pulse in the veins in my neck was visible to the naked eye. That's never a good sign! Beyond that, the embarrassment factor was incredible. From that day to this John has never missed a chance to dig me up about it, sometimes bringing it up in conversation with total strangers. This state of affairs will only change if and when John has his very own planning disaster. It's nice to have something to look forward to.

John; It was a lovely run up through Ayrshire, and we saw a fabulous sunset over Arran. It was braw. This was the second longest day of the year, and a beauty.

The only problem on the train was enjoying our cans without the ticket person seeing us, although I am certain he didn't give a shit. In fact he sneaked up behind me once in full swally.

Funny thing about the timing of the train was that if we got off our train in Ayr, waited 10 minutes and got on another train which stopped at about six more stops than the one we were on, we would get into Glasgow about half an hour sooner than if we stayed on the one we were on which was also going to Glasgow. Hope you can understand what I'm trying to say.

So we got off in Ayr and on to the other train. The guard on this train didn't care about us having a can either.

We got off the train in The Central Station and wandered over and onto the EK train without Craig mentioning a visit to *"The Horseshoe"*, our normal stopping off pub in Glasgow on our way home. I think he was worried it might be shut.

Craig's Irene was at EK station and ran us home. I've said it before, but what a woman, and lucky too.

So ended a great day out. The chance to slag off Craig made the day even better than normal.

In Summary

Our epic trek down south was a bit of a new experience for us. New in that we were denied our basic rights: draught beer.

Dumfries is a good place to spend an hour or two, especially if you find yourself in The World's End.

One of the big mistakes we made that day, and there were many, was to omit Castle Douglas from our plans. It's a nice place to visit, with much to occupy the tourist. But more importantly it also has a few really good drinking establishments, which is more than can be said about some of our planned stops.

Gatehouse of Fleet and Creetown were a bit of a disappointment from our point of view, but they are quite picturesque and might appeal to the travelling teetotaller.

Newton Stewart on the other hand is well equipped with hostelries, and they are open for business.

So apart from a bit of a dip in the middle section this trip turned out well.

Rothesay, it's a Wee Bute

(Fae Mac's tae the Golfers then oan to the Cri
These pubs are jist magic an' that is nae lie)

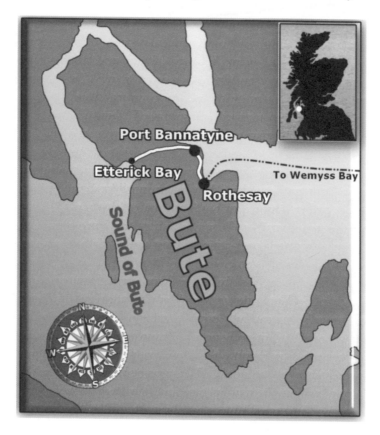

East Kilbride-Ettrick Bay-Port Bannatyne-
Rothesay-East Kilbride
Four Buses-Four Trains-Two Ferries

Rothesay, it's a Wee Bute

John; This trip was only thought of by me a few days before we went. But it was such an obvious and important one that I am amazed neither of us thought of it before. For people of our age, Rothesay is better known and loved than anywhere else in the West of Scotland, and I doubt if there is anyone over 60 who's not visited the Island. Well that's my opinion anyway. More importantly, there are literally dozens of pubs on the Island of Bute, although a few have closed because of the recession in the last two or three years. It is also my favourite place in Scotland. So I organized the trip, spread sheet and everything, and a more colourful spreadsheet than the one Craig produced for our last trip. He said it was tacky.

So at 9.30a.m., on a sunny Wednesday morning, I collected Craig and we wandered across the Murray Road, got on the old 201 which took us to Hairmyres Station.

Before getting on the train, Craig bought a roll and sausage from the wee kiosk at the station, the smell of Creish attracted him (Creish is Ayrshire for grease). He said it was hard and tasted of cardboard. He had already had his breakfast so it served him right.

It was a lovely sunny day (the second this year) and we enjoyed the train journey into Glasgow. We had to sit facing the back of the train. Craig hates sitting this way. Between the backward thing and the crap roll, I was enjoying the start to the day, Craig was getting depressed. He thought everything was against him, or in the case of the train, behind him. He cheered up a bit when he remembered he had heard on the Scottish travel news that there were signal problems at Paisley Gilmour Street Station which was causing delays. If there was a delay and we missed my planned ferry, that would cheer him up after all the slagging I gave him for his screw-ups in the last trip which he had organized.

Craig; *While sitting in planning HQ one night (The Crooked Lum that is) we decided that we had made a major error in not*

109

exploring the many delights Rothesay has to offer. To be honest John did all the deciding. He is obsessed with the place it has to be said. He spent much of his childhood on the island and talks about it constantly.

Rothesay, the main town on the island of Bute, is the kind of place where you could either spend a lot of time wandering around just taking in the sights or, like us, head straight to one of the many fine pubs in the town. The town used to be a major seaside resort playing host to a huge number of holiday makers from the West of Scotland. Its economy was firmly based on tourism. Many families would spend their entire holiday there staying in one of its many small hotels or guest houses. There was also always a healthy trade in day trippers.

Times have changed however and Rothesay, like so many other Scottish seaside resorts has suffered a huge loss in popularity. It can still be a great destination for a day out, it's just not so busy anymore. Many attempts to revitalise the town have been made over the years.

A new marina has been built and the ferries have been upgraded. Mount Stuart House is open to the public and is highly recommended by tourist organisations. If you enjoy looking at displays of conspicuous opulence achieved at the expense of generations of poorly paid, peasant workers I can highly recommend it myself. My personal favourite piece of redevelopment in Rothesay is the Victorian lavatories, apparently it really drew in the crowds when they first opened, but as numbers declined a little this allowed the odd cynic to claim that the whole operation had been a flash in the pan.

We have already travelled around the other two main islands of the Firth of Clyde. Arran and Great Cumbrae had proved to be really good days out with plenty to see and a good number of pubs to visit. Bute seemed ripe for a visit.

Anyway, we have visited the town a few times in the past but only as a refreshment stop on one of our longer journeys. This

110

time we decided to concentrate our efforts on visiting as many of the town's watering holes as possible.

The town has an incredible ratio of pubs to punters, with about 20 offering refreshment to the weary traveller. I was very impressed when I found this out. According to John there is an amusing form of social mobility to be found in Rothesay these days. That is to say that a lot of the town's social drinkers like to get mobile of an evening. They like to do the rounds of a few pubs rather than stick to just the one. I suppose this wide distribution of the alcohol pound is what keeps so many of the places open. God bless them.

A less charitable person might suggest that the reason why they visit so many different pubs is so that no one knows just how many drinks they manage to put away of an evening. It doesn't do to let too many people know your business when you live on a small island. Rumour is a currency in small communities.

Many people, including myself, forget that Rothesay is the name of the town and not the island. The same thing happens with Millport/Cumbrae. It must drive the locals crazy.

There was of course another reason for our visit. John had decided that Bute would have the honour of being the first outlet for the sale of our first literary masterpiece 'The Cheap Way Round'. At the time of writing this piece we are still waiting to see just how honoured the good folks of the island feel about that. It has been suggested, by me one night after a particularly intense meeting, that we should be targeting the likes of 'Waterstone's to sell our book. Less charitable friends have suggested the 'Pound Shop' might be a more realistic option.

John; There were no real delays and we had a lovely run down the side of the Clyde to Wemyss Bay Station, one of the nicest stations in Scotland, at least it would be if the council would give it some money to allow it to put up the hanging baskets the way it used to do. If they would just accept more gifts like the organizers of the commonwealth games, there would be plenty of money for the nice flowers.

We wandered down the lovely concourse and got our ferry tickets. Because it was a day return, we got an old person's discount which was only about 10%. What a shower of miserable bastards the Scottish Parliament are. Mind you, the free travel on the buses is magic, so I won't go on too much.

Craig wasn't keen on sitting outside, so we sat at the front of the ferry, inside. Craig's not a real sailor like me.

The sail over to Rothesay, in the sunshine, was magic. What a lovely place the Firth of Clyde is. The ferry moored at 12.35p.m., and we wandered up to Guildford Square to catch the West Coast 490 bus to Ettrick Bay. The reason for going there is that we have now printed about 50 copies of our first book, "The Cheap Way Round", and we are starting to try to sell it through small book shops and touristy places. We have had no luck yet in getting a publisher, but we are still trying.

Craig; We set off for Bute at about 9.30am. with a supply of crisp new books in my rucksack. While we waited for our train at Hairmyres I unwisely decided to have a quick snack from the station café. It was a nice enough place and very probably had an extensive menu of delicious, well cooked, meals. Unfortunately I had square sausage in mind. To her credit the girl behind the counter did ask if I wanted sauce with my roll on square. What I didn't realise was what she was actually asking was 'Do you want flavour with that?' The thing was tasteless! I might as well have been chewing on a lump of lukewarm, corrugated cardboard. That was the first but unfortunately not the last disappointment of the day.

On the boat over to Rothesay I had to insist that we knock back a couple of beers just to keep us going. This was an act of necessity due to a bit of suspect planning by John. He had arranged for us to visit Ettrick Bay which, as any visitor to Bute would know, has no pub or hotel. In fact it doesn't have

112

very much of anything. We had been on about twenty or so trips to many parts of the country by the time this one came around. The one constant in all of them had been an easy access to quantities of thirst quenching alcohol. It's a theme. John seemed to think it was hilarious that we were stuck there for an hour. It would appear that he was under the impression that I didn't know that Ettrick Bay was publess. In fact I had been there twice before. Admittedly one of those times was by accident. I'd gotten lost. That in itself is a bit of an achievement given that there are only a couple of roads on the island.

The Ettrick Bay bus keeps right on to the end of the road.

John; There is a lovely café at Ettrick bay which, as well as great food, sells some books of local interest, so we thought we'd chance our arm. Craig was up for it as long as I did the bullshit stuff, which I've done all my working life. What I had failed to tell him was that the place had no license so he had an hour to kill till the next bus without a bevy, and it was about one o'clock by then. But it was the same for me.

The man who owned the café/restaurant liked the book and took six. He also asked me to come back next time I was down as he reckoned he'd sell them. We were so happy Craig forgot he was still sober.

We felt we couldn't just bugger off without buying something so we both had a plate of soup. It was delicious, best soup (apart from Kate's) I've ever tasted. After the soup we walked along the front of the bay and found a lovely seat facing the water and had our pieces. Great start to the day. Ettrick Bay is a lovely place, but more important matters (bevy) awaited.

The two o'clock bus, the West Coast 90 took us to our next port of call, Port Bannatyne, a place famous for looking lovely from a distance, with loads of yachts and hanging baskets. It also has its fair share of jakies and druggies. Mind you, so has everywhere else. By the way, if Port Bannatyne can find the money for hanging baskets, why can't Wemyss Bay Station?

But I digress, I knew there were at least three pubs still open but must admit to panic when the first two were shut, Craig could smell revenge for my slagging him off during the last trip. The third one, *"The Anchor Tavern"*, was thankfully open, and what a great wee pub it was. The beer was great and the locals and barmaid Ilene, were great fun. They all had a read of our book, but nobody showed any interest in buying one. You can't blame them with the price of bevy nowadays.

A wee bloke at the end of the bar was from Durham, and although he had lived on the Island for about 20 years, had a very broad Durham accent and we had a hell of a problem understanding a word he said. We just had to resort to answers like 'your right there wee man', and 'you never said a truer word', whatever the f*** tit word was (good Yorkshire patter, I think). We hoped he didn't take offence if we gave the wrong reply.

Then a girl walked in, and without introducing herself, started telling us and everybody in the pub a story about how she had just burned a hole in her arse when a tube of lighter fuel was set alight in her pocket while she was on her boat (she effd' and blinded her way through the story). I said I didn't believe her, but she refused to show me her arse, although she didn't put it as nice as that.

We had a great time with the locals and the arse burner, but all too soon had to leave to get our next bus, another West Coast 90, into Guildford Square in Rothesay.

Barman Rating; 🍺🍺🍺🍺🍺

Craig; Anyway, we had a pleasant, if sober, time wandering around the bay. The last time I had visited this place the only interesting thing to be seen there was a wrecked boat which had run aground on the beach some years ago. Since my last visit It had apparently been salvaged or whatever they call it when they take away the only thing worth looking at. We now had an unrestricted view of not very much at all.

We did have a very nice lunch in the café there. It was very busy but we were served quickly by an efficient and friendly waitress. That's not a sentence you will often see applied to a Scottish food outlet.

I have to admit that it was the thought of a good session in the two or three pubs of Port Bannatyne that kept me going during my enforced stay in Ettrick Bay. Little did I know that we were speeding towards another disappointment when we eventually caught the bus back into town.

Port Bannatyne seemed to be having a day off. I was a little surprised to find the place so run down. A couple of years ago it was announced that a new marina was to be built there. This kind of development usually means that a lot of money gets spent tarting up the area. Cafés and trendy bars springing up all over the place are the usual by-product of marina developments. Obviously no one told the people of Port Bannatyne. There were quite a few boats tied up at the quay but there wasn't a hint of any gentrification going on. In fact there were hardly any signs of life.

The pub I was most looking forward to visiting was 'The Port Royal Hotel. It is apparently a Russian Tavern. I'm not entirely sure what difference that makes, but I wanted to find out. The thought occurred to me that apart from selling a lot of cabbage based foodstuffs a Russian pub would be remarkably similar to a bad Scottish one. The staff would be cold, unhelpful and aggressive.

**The barmaid had an unfortunate accident.
You could say it was a bit o' a bummer!**

The door was open, but only just. We couldn't see or hear any signs of activity in the place and decided it must be closed. Things were not looking good.

116

Rothesay, it's a Wee Bute

The only other pub we could find to visit in the 'Port' didn't look too lively either. The Anchor Tavern looked dark. By this time we were getting desperate. It had been almost two hours since we had last tasted beer. Open for business or not we were going in. Fortunately it was open and we took full advantage of that.

It took a little while for our eyes to adjust to the low lighting in the bar. Low light levels in older pubs are not usually a good sign. Very often there are good reasons for keeping the lights down. Believe me we have supped beer in some right middens in our on-going quest for the perfect pint. Keeping the wattage low can cover a multitude of sins. From bad decorating choices to the odd patch of mysterious mould creeping up the wall, we have seen them all.

The Anchor didn't suffer from any of these ailments so I can only imagine that the owners are on a bit of an economy drive. We enjoyed a couple of pints and a bit of banter with the staff and customers. John tried his now standard ploy of mentioning 'the book' in the hope of getting a free pint. Once again he failed miserably. There were four other people in the bar, including the barmaid. The young couple sitting behind us seemed quite interested in the book as did the barmaid. I had high hopes of a sale. Needless to say no one bought a copy of the book. Although it is quite possible the strange Geordie bloke wanted to buy one but we couldn't understand a word he was saying. He was either trying to buy us a pint, buy a book or challenge us to fight. We will never know.

Just before we left the pub the other barmaid came in. She was hilarious. Apparently she had just burned her nether regions with a cigarette. From the language she was using I think chewing tobacco would have been more appropriate for her. She may, or may not have had a blister on her bum, but she could certainly blister paint with her language.

Rothesay, it's a Wee Bute

John; The weekend before this trip, Kate and I had been in Rothesay for a couple of days and had a night out with friends of ours, Ian and Dierdrie, who had bought our book and had the idea of getting Craig and I to sign it. So on hearing we were planning a trip to Rothesay in a few days, she came up with the idea of coming up to us on the street, kidding on she didn't know me and say she had just bought the book in a local shop, which had also taken books last week, and thought she recognized us from the cover, and ask us to sign the book for us. These ideas sound great after six gin and tonics.

So she came up to us in Guildford Square, did her act of not knowing me, and Craig fell for it hook, line and sinker, He was so chuffed he got me to photograph them together, what a laugh. But to tell the truth, I was starting to feel guilty about taking the piss out of Craig. When the photographic session was finished, and we were saying our goodbyes', we owned up to Craig, who gave the impression of taking it in good spirit. I have my doubts though, for Craig comes from Auchinleck, where memories are long, and taking the piss is not forgotten or forgiven, so I'm sleeping with the light on from now on.

Craig's mood brightened when we went into the book shop in Rothesay and the lady who owned the shop had a look through the book and said she'd take six copies. We were really pleased. Craig started talking about who would appear in the movie of the book.

We wandered up to what we hoped would be our first of many Rothesay pubs, *"Macs Bar"*. Mac's is a great wee bar and the barman and the couple of locals who were in were all great company and a great laugh. Unfortunately, the owner was not in, and I think he wanted to buy a book. Not to worry as they were going like hotcakes.

The only thing about the pub is that it now has three huge tellies, instead of the old one it used to have. To be fair, mind you, the locals said it is great for watching three matches at the one time. It must cost the owner a fortune. The locals all said it was great.

A tremendously interesting thing about the old telly is that it had been on the wall for over 17 years and was on for about 12 hours a day and never had given a problem in all that time.

We were having a great time in 'Mac's, but I was worried that Sheila, Kate's sister, who lives on the Island, and knew we were coming to the island that day would be wanting to join us. Sheila is a real party animal and there was no way of stopping her (and we tried). My mobile rang and I knew she had found us. She asked why I hadn't answered her texts. I told her that I hadn't received any. She didn't believe me. I admitted we were in 'Mac's Bar', but that we wanted to visit another couple of pubs before we met up with her. She pretended this was ok although I knew she was gagging for a bevy. We agreed to meet up at some time, I think about five o'clock, in the 'Taverna', which is a more suitable pub for ladies to visit (thought I would call Sheila a lady to cheer her up).

Barman Rating;

Craig ; Back in Rothesay we got off the bus in Guilford Square and stepped into a right bit of nonsense. As we crossed the road I was accosted by a strange woman. She started going on about the book and how she had just bought it. Apparently it was all supposed to be a hilarious prank. I didn't get it. To be honest I think the woman must have some sort of attention seeking disorder. That's a kind way of saying she must be barking. Then again you just can't get the care in the community these days. Eventually she toddled off, possibly to get her medication, and we got on with the business of the day. We had visited Mac's Bar earlier in the year and had a very nice time there, hence this 'official' visit. Sometimes it's just not a great idea to revisit a favourite place. The chances are that you will never be able to recreate that moment. That was certainly the case here. The owner, who had been a laugh a

minute the last time, was busy elsewhere. His replacement was
a bit more economic with the chuckling. In fact very little
seemed to please him. Certainly not our book anyway!
John's sister-in-law managed to make contact with us in Mac's
Bar. She phoned John to make arrangements to meet up. There
were some whispered allegations about the illegal use of
tracking devices, but we both knew it had only been a matter of
time before she traced us. I had a feeling that our fact finding
trip was about to turn into a drinking session.

John; We left the nice atmosphere of 'Mac's and wandered
down High Street, along the front and into *'The Golfers'*. It
was completely empty when we went in but the barman,
Tommy, was singing along, very loudly, to all the songs that
were blasting out from somewhere. In the old days it would be
from a juke box, but nowadays you never know where it is
coming from, so you can't turn it off. It was also impossible to
turn Tommy off. We had had about three pints by then and
were on our fourth so Tommy started to sound all right. During
a break in the music we managed to have a quick chat with him
and he is a great wee guy. The only problem with the pub was
that it was empty. We said goodbye to Tommy and wandered
back outside to enjoy the view of the harbour.

Barman Rating; 🍺🍺🍺🍺

It was only a couple of steps to our next pub, *'The Palace'*. I
don't know why I decided to take Craig here as I knew it is a
pretty depressing place and is normally a watering hole for
people even older than us. We had a quick pint and got out as
quickly as possible without insulting the barmaid or the locals.

Barman Rating; 🍺🍺

'The Criterion', or *'The Cri '* to the locals was the last pub we
would have time to visit before our rendezvous with the girls.
This is a pub with good atmosphere and a friendly barman
called Tommy, I think. We had a great pint and enjoyed a chat
with Tommy. But all too soon the time was approaching five

o'clock and our meeting with Sheila. So we said goodbye to Tommy and wandered back along the front, admiring the gardens and palm trees.

Barman Rating; █ █ █ █

Craig; Before meeting up with Sheila we paid a visit to 'The Golfers'. Even before we got into the pub we could hear the singing, slightly deranged singing. It turned out that the barman, Tommy, was alone in the bar and was just singing to amuse himself.

Neil Diamond was Tommy's artist of choice to duet with and, from what we could hear, there is absolutely no reason to alert Simon Cowell. We spent a little time chatting to the barman about the decline in the number of public houses on the island. Given that the Golfer's is a popular pub and was totally empty, apart from two intrepid pub reviewers, it is easy to see why so many pubs are closing, and not just in Rothesay.

Once again John tried, and failed, to flog our book to the bartender. Perhaps it was this failure which clouded his judgement when he was choosing our next place to visit. Something strange certainly got into his head.

The Palace Bar was obviously named by someone who likes a bit of irony. A less likely palace I could not imagine. I did get a little bit nostalgic when I noticed the 1960s formica bar top. We didn't hang around very long as we felt a wee bit out of place. Being the youngest people in there, and not being clinically depressed we did stand out from the crowd, such as it was.

The Criterion was our next watering hole and it was worth putting up with the dross we had just suffered to get to this little gem. The pub just felt right the moment we walked in the door. It is slightly old fashioned, but that's the way it's supposed to be. There has obviously been a lot of effort put into the upkeep of this bar.

The beer was good and the owner, Ian, is a bit of a character. We were treated to a concise history of Rothesay's pubs and, depending on your sense of humour, a couple of funny stories. Usually we have one pint per pub, but we were enjoying the craic so much that we decided to squeeze in an extra brew. Not being the heroic types, we settled on the idea of half pints. After all we had to meet up with Sheila, a woman you don't want to keep waiting.

John parting with cash, an unmissable
photo opportunity!

John; We wandered along the prom and into the *'Taverna'*, and that was when the party really started. Sheila had told me that her pal, Irish Suzie, who I knew, and who drinks as much as Sheila, was going to meet us there.

By the way, Irish Suzie is called 'Irish' because she's from Northern Ireland. These islanders have some imagination. Wonder what they'd call her if she came from Southern Ireland, never mind.

Suzie arrived on time and we had a great time, and a right good few rounds. *"The Taverna"* is one of the best pubs in Rothesay and the staff and beer are great.

Barman and Barmaid Ratings; 🍺🍺🍺🍺🍺

To be honest, the rest of the journey was a bit of a blur. I remember we sat outside at the back of the ferry and enjoyed a pint as the evening sun beat down on us. It was magic, I think. We got the train back to Glasgow, slept all the way, got off and right onto the East Kilbride train. No nicking into *"The Horseshoe"* for a pint as we normally do. This sensible behaviour went out of the window when, sobering up, we arrived in East Kilbride. Craig, or was it me, decided we needed a small refreshment before facing the wives. So it was into *"The Monty"* for a couple of pints. Will we never learn?

Irene picked us up, she is either a glutton for punishment, or she might feel it is the only way she'll get Craig home. He is more of a nighthawk than me and would stay out all night if he was allowed.

So another day of fun and bevy, with a few book sales on top, was over. Rothesay is not as busy as it once was, but when the sun is shining there is no more beautiful place.

Craig; We left 'The Cri', and Ian's unique sense of humour, and made our way to the Taverna. It's a nice enough pub and the clientele seemed quite friendly but, it wasn't what I was looking for. I prefer a place with a bit of character.

We were still at our first drink when a real character walked in. Actually hobbled in would be a better description. Irish Suzie made a dramatic entrance. She is a driven woman and the fuel she uses is alcohol.

123

Earlier that day she had twisted her ankle. Her foot was now the size of a rugby ball. But this minor inconvenience didn't seem to be holding her back to any noticeable degree. I'm fairly sure that she would be more than capable of crawling over broken glass if it meant she could get her hands on a good bevy.

The rest of our session in the Taverna followed an exact pattern. Suzie and Sheila drank and talked while we drank and listened. We knew the game was up and surrendered without a whimper. They wouldn't have heard us anyway.

On the boat back over to Wemyss Bay we sat up top drinking a couple of beers, in total silence. That was a real treat after the ear bashing we had been through in Rothesay.

John showed great restraint in Glasgow Central. He was a bit twitchy as we made our way straight to the platform for the East Kilbride train. He doesn't like to miss out on a chance to visit the Horse Shoe Bar if he finds himself anywhere in or near the city centre. By the time we got to East Kilbride he was champing at the bit for a couple of cold brews. I thought it only fair to join him.

It had been a very strange day for us. First of all I had nearly poisoned myself with a suspect roll which may or may not have contained a vintage piece of meat flavoured cardboard. Actually the jury is still out on whether any meat was involved in the making of that particular item. And, although we had delivered the books we were carrying to the shops, we had been a bit side tracked by outside influences. That would be influences of the in-law variety.

But we take our roles as conscientious analysts of all things relating to a good day out on the batter very seriously and I think we carried out our duty rather well, yet again.

In Summary

If you are looking for a good old fashioned, traditional family holiday you could do a lot worse than take a trip 'doon the watter' to Rothesay.

There is a frequent ferry service to the town, with the trip lasting around thirty minutes or so. With a connecting train to Glasgow Central it's easy to reach for a holiday or a wee day trip.

The Isle of Bute has a lot to offer the determined holidaymaker. For them that can be bothered there is a castle, a country house with ornamental gardens, golf and of course an awful lot of scenery. In fact there's enough going on there to keep you out of the pub for hours on end.

Rothesay could easily become the pub crawl capital of Western Scotland. It has, as they say, more pubs than you could shake a stick at.

We didn't have the time or the constitution to visit them all, but we gave it our best shot.

On the whole there were very few disappointments on our trip. All the buses, trains and boats arrived and left on time. And, of course, the pubs were really good. In fact Rothesay came out top of our list for good bar service with a score of 4 out of 5 on the Russell Standard.

Away for a Wee Paddle

(The sun may shine, the wind may blow
But if more than a breeze the Waverley'll no go.)

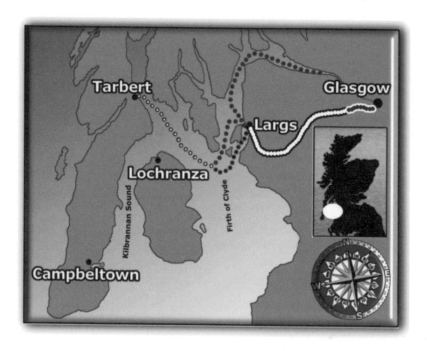

(One Waverley, Two Trains, One Taxi)

John; Since we started doing these trips, Craig and I have been trying to include Campbeltown in one of them. As most of you know it is situated at the end of The Mull of Kintyre (made famous by Andy Stewart singing 'Campbeltown Loch I wish you were Whisky'), long before Paul McCartney was a star.

To get to Campbeltown, visit several pubs, and get back in a day can be done, but we would not have time to go anywhere else, and god knows how I would survive about four hours in a bus after several pints. As you know, toilets are not guaranteed on buses, and if there is one, it might not be working.

So can you imagine our delight, when we discovered that 'The Waverley' was sailing to Campbeltown on the 17th of July. There was no holding us back. A sail on 'The Waverley' has always been on our agenda, and although you are talking about over £30, it is a must for men of our age. By the way, £30 includes a good wee saving for us pensioners.

So the plan, after much discussion, was to sail from Glasgow, via Largs and Lochranza, to Campbeltown, where we would have about two and a half hours ashore.

This would give us enough time to visit several pubs in the town.

I was a bit worried that as soon as the Waverley sets sail from Glasgow, which was to be 9am, the bars open. This would give us about five hours drinking time before our arrival at Campbeltown.

When I said I was a bit worried about the bars opening as soon as the boat left, who am I kidding. What I actually meant was that I was delighted the bars would be opening straight away.

Craig had two huge concerns, the first was that there is always someone on the boat playing an accordion, and for some reason Craig hates the accordion. The last time we were on 'The Waverley' he was trapped in a corner with the musician belting out Jimmy Shand for hours right in his face, what a laugh. His second worry was that the last time we sailed (and this was about six years ago) he was all excited that we were going to stop in Islay, where he had never been before. As we approached the island, the skipper announced it was too windy to dock, so he missed his much anticipated visit to Islay. Remembering that Auchinleck men hold grudges forever, I was a bit concerned.

The main reason for this concern was that after about a week of great weather, the forecast was for gale force winds and rain all day in one of the areas we were sailing to. That's right, Campbeltown.

However, with that worry in my mind, which I knew would disappear after about three pints, we set off from my house.

Craig; This particular trip had the potential to be one of our best so far. A trip on the Waverley is always a great day out. The very mention of its name is enough to bring a tear to even the most cynical traveller's eye. Presuming, of course, that said traveller is male and over 40 years of age.

The MV Waverley is the last ocean going paddle steamer in the world and every summer it plies its trade in the waters off the west coast of Scotland.

Since we started travelling round Scotland it has always been an ambition of ours to work in a trip aboard the Waverley. That hasn't been easy. I think it was John who came up with a plan which would make that small dream of ours come true. He's taking credit for it anyway.

There have been problems putting a plan together which would include the ship. Not least of them was the cost of a trip aboard the Waverley. Basically, when you're writing a book about travelling on the cheap, shelling out a fortune on a wee sail around the Clyde seems a bit extravagant. It would be cheaper to fly to Campbeltown than sail there on this boat. Well it would be if Ryanair had a service to the area.

We have been trying to organise a trip to Campbeltown for some time. A trip there would be the longest journey we had ever attempted. There is a coach which would take us all the way from Glasgow to Campbeltown. The Citylink 926 takes more than four hours to make the journey. Ideally we would like to break that journey to squeeze in a couple of extra refreshment stops and, of course, take in the sights. That would however leave us with very little time in Campbeltown itself. The alternative would be an overnight stay which would be a bit on the expensive side.

The discovery, by John apparently, that for one day only the Waverley would be calling at Campbeltown was an answer to our planning dilemma. There was, as ever, a drawback. The one day it was scheduled to call in at the port was a Sunday. This complicated things once more. There are always travel problems on Sundays, it is Scotland after all. Our first plan was to take the bus, or rather buses, to Campbeltown. Then, after a good look around the town and of course a couple of beers we would take the Waverley back to Glasgow. The advantage to this plan was that not only did the Waverley have extensive toilet facilities, a god send for those of us with suspect bladder control, but it had two rather fine bars aboard. This plan had everything we could want. In fact it was too good to be true. Because we had to depend on a Sunday schedule on the buses the plan had no chance. There are not too many local buses in the Kintyre area at the best of times. On a Sunday there didn't seem to be any.

Another problem was that we couldn't book a single ticket journey on the Waverley. That meant we would have to take a chance that there would be room for us on the ship after all the returning passengers were on board. This didn't seem like a risk worth taking. Being marooned in Campbeltown on a wet and windy Sunday doesn't bear thinking about.

Our second option was never really viable. We could take the Waverley from Glasgow directly to Campbeltown, then make the return journey by bus. It was too impractical. The Sunday bus problem would still be there and of course, even if we could get on the bus, it's a long way back to Glasgow. John, and his bladder, might not make it.

We eventually settled for option C, the easy option. A round trip on our favourite boat would surely mean nothing could possibly go wrong, could it? It might not fit in with our ethos of travelling on the cheap but, on the other hand, ye cannie beat a wee booze cruise.

John; My wife, the lovely and lucky Kate, said she would run us to the terminal in Glasgow. This was a tremendous gesture as it meant she would have to be up at seven, and we were having a late night the night before, babysitting.

Craig asked if Tam, a friend of his from his Auchinleck days, could come on the trip with us. This was no problem as I have met Tam several times and he is a great bloke.

As he lives, more or less, on the way to the terminal, we picked him up and arrived at the terminal at about quarter to nine.

Despite the crap forecast, there was a big queue to get on, and the sun was out. It was lovely. These weather forecasters have no idea.

As we left the Science Museum Terminal in Glasgow, Craig and Tam suggested we check out one of the bars before we had too much to drink, this was 9am. For some reason this seemed to make sense to me, so we went downstairs, had a look at the engines, which are fantastic, and went into the bar and had just the one pint. The pints were good and the place was very nice and comfy, with great views out of the windows.

We finished our pints and wandered up on deck and passed famous, and great places like Partick, Govan, Linthouse, Whiteinch, Clydebank, Renfrew and then down to Dumbarton. Although most of the shipyards are closed, it is still a great trip, and a nostalgic one for the older people on the boat, which means just about everyone.

Away for a Wee Paddle

The highlights of the first part of the river was a seaplane flying overhead (we are easy to please). We then passed Clydebank College, where Tam was a lecturer for many years. In fact he had just retired in the last few days and took great pleasure in waving goodbye to it from the river. Seemed to me he was waving with only two fingers, although I might be mistaken.

Craig; *It was an early start for us but we were lucky to be getting a lift down to the quay at Glasgow Science Centre. Kate had volunteered to take us. John thought she was being very kind. My take on it was that it shows just how desperate she was to get him out of the house. We had arranged to have an old pal of mine join us on this trip. He was taking early retirement and we thought it would be a good way to celebrate the occasion.*

After picking Tam up in Pollokshields we arrived at the Centre with about half an hour to spare. There was a bit of a queue waiting to get aboard, but nowhere as long as I thought it would be. It seemed to me that we passengers might be outnumbered by the crew. Obviously some would-be travellers had seen the weather forecast for the Firth of Clyde and decided not to tempt fate. We were made of sterner stuff.

I was stunned to learn that my friend of more years than I'm prepared to talk about, Tam, had never in his entire life been on the Waverley; unbelievable!

Since both John (seawater in the veins) Mackay and I were seasoned mariners, and we had an uninitiated guest traveller with us we decided to give him the deluxe tour of the Waverley. This entailed staring at the engines for five minutes before adjourning to the bar. It's a tradition, for men of a certain age, to stand beside the engines drooling at the sight of all that gleaming engineering. The movement of it all is quite hypnotic. In the bar we paid an obscene amount of money for three quite reasonable pints. As we sat carefully sipping our very expensive brews, to make them last longer, we smugly congratulated ourselves for being ever so smart. We had wisely packed a healthy supply of canned beer in our rucksacks. We were going to save a fortune.

John; As we approached Port Glasgow and Greenock we thought it was a good opportunity to nick downstairs and check out the lower bar. This is a great wee bar with porthole windows right on the waterline. The bar was very quiet but we enjoyed the pints as we watched the water go by.

If you ask me this crew are definitely looking a wee bit scurvy.

Tam and I went back up on deck when the captain announced that we were passing a cruise ship which was moored in Greenock. It was one of the 'Holland America Line' ships. The captain said that it was not scheduled to be in Greenock, but the weather was so wild in Oban, where they should have been,

132

that they had to come to Greenock. What a bummer for the passengers.

Oban is called 'The Gateway to the Islands' and is a beautiful place. Greenock is something else altogether. Mind you, the passengers would have had a lovely sail up the Firth of Clyde. We went back down to join Craig, who was looking after the pints. We finished ours, and went back up on deck, found a nice seat at the stern (back) and enjoyed the sail down the firth to Largs in lovely sunshine. It was magic. Think we had our first can on the sail to Largs. By the way, you're not supposed to bring drink onto the boat as they've plenty to sell you on board, although, like everywhere else, it's a hell of a price.

Craig; When the boat approached the pier in Largs I could see that there were about a couple of hundred people waiting to get on. Everything was looking good for a great day's cruising. The captain had other ideas unfortunately.

I had a bad feeling when his voice came over the tannoy. At first he said we might not make it to Campbeltown because of possible bad weather. If we couldn't make it, he continued, we would just put in at Lochranza on the north coast of Arran.

I suggested that we jump ship there and then, before we left the safety of Largs pier. Having been stuck in Lochranza some time ago I was in no hurry to go back there. To describe it as a one horse town would be to grossly exaggerate its importance. There is one hotel in the village and I didn't fancy our chances of getting a pint in it when another two or three hundred thirsty souls turned up at the bar.

I was over ruled by my two shipmates. Presumably they have never had the opportunity to sample the delights on offer in the north of Arran.

As it turned out we were all spared that ordeal. Our fearless captain had decided that Lochranza was off the chart and we would now be going to Tarbert. I was greatly relieved. Tarbert has a fair few pubs in it.

133

John; Largs was lovely in the sunshine and there was a big crowd waiting to board. Although the weather at this stage was lovely, by the time we were about to leave the wind seemed to get up and the water was becoming choppy, but not bad.

Before we left Largs, the Captain announced that he had been in contact with the people in Campbeltown and there were strong winds and the forecast was that they would get worse. He then said he might have to cancel the Campbeltown visit but, hopefully, we could still get to Lochranza and then do a sail from there. He would keep us informed. Craig was just starting to think the world was against him.

He might be rubbish at pole dancing
But it keeps him happy.

Away for a Wee Paddle

He didn't believe for a minute that the weather was that bad and thought that the captain was just doing this to annoy him, and it worked.

If this wasn't bad enough, an accordion player suddenly appeared and started playing pretty badly it has to be said, right in front of us. It was hysterical. Craig was even more raging. I asked Craig if he had any change to give the musician. I can't write down his reply.

We cruised round the south end of the beautiful Island of Bute and over to the north end of Arran. To be fair to the captain, the weather to the south was looking pretty grim, but this was no consolation to Craig.

Craig; A large group of passengers who had just come aboard in Largs were even more relieved than me about our change of destination. It seems they were on a coach tour of Scotland and were supposed to meet up with their bus again in Campbeltown. As all their luggage was now hurtling towards that town aboard their coach they had been less than pleased by the prospect of a wee trip to Arran. At least by getting off in Tarbert they stood a reasonable chance of meeting up with their suitcases again. We are all quite used to airlines misplacing our luggage but I doubt it happens too often on Clyde steamers nowadays.

My happiness at our change of destination was short lived however. I really should know better by now. Good news is always followed by bad.

My particular dark cloud came in the form of a tone deaf accordionist. Actually he might not have been tone deaf, maybe it's just because I hate accordions. I am extremely grateful that Scotland adopted the bagpipes as its national instrument rather than the dreaded accordion. Imagine what a terrible place this would be if that were the case. The massed accordions and drums of the Argyll and Sutherland Highlanders just doesn't bear thinking about. Anyway, he took up position about twenty feet away from me and proceeded to murder Scotland's musical heritage. To my untrained ear it sounded as if he was wearing boxing gloves while playing.

John; The Captain made a further announcement letting us know that we would not be going to Campbeltown or Lochranza because of the windy weather, but we were going to cruise up into Loch Fyne and stop at Tarbert for a couple of hours, as there was no windy weather up there.

We felt this was better than being stuck in Lochranza, which unless you are an Aran sweater wearing, hiking sort of person, is a bit of a nothing sort of place, but pretty to look at.

So with Campbeltown out of the window, we sat back to enjoy a couple of cans, and the scenery, which was lovely, but we all agreed you can only look at nice scenery for a couple of minutes without becoming bored out of your skull.

We landed at Tarbert about 3.15pm and were told to be back on board by 5.15pm or we would be left behind. Tarbert is a lovely place to look at, but you wouldn't want to be stuck there.

It was about a 10 minute walk into the town and we fairly belted along the front and were one of the first of the passengers to arrive. I think Craig was worried they'd run out of drink.

Craig; As soon as we got ashore on Tarbert, the three of us, pursued by a hundred or so fellow passengers, made a beeline for the far end of the town. That's where they keep the pubs.

I've been in 'The Corner House' so often over the last few years that the barman thinks I'm a local. It's a good pub and the beer is fine. What more could a weary seafarer ask for? My two companions were all for settling down for the duration, but I reminded them that we had a job to do.

Outside there was a barge moored at the quayside. It was some sort of floating bar. Actually it looked a bit upmarket for the likes of us. And it was. John decided to go aboard anyway, to

check what beer was on offer. He was back in seconds. They
didn't stoop to selling draught beer apparently.
Fortunately I thought I knew where we could find a good wee
bar; I remembered it from a previous visit. The Back Bar is
actually part of The Tarbert Hotel and I had enjoyed a pint or
two in it about two years before.
As soon as I opened the door I could sense something had
changed. I remembered it as a wee bit of a dive. It had been
quite dark and old fashioned and its customers were a bit
grungy as well. Two old codgers were shouting what sounded
like nonsense at each other and a younger man was playing the
bandit. Every now and then he would head butt the machine
and swear at it. In other words it was very atmospheric and
made me come over all nostalgic for my own old home town.
I had been looking forward to John and Tam's reaction to the
place, but it was now so different. The bar had been done up. It
was now modern, clean and shiny. I was so disappointed.
The clientele had also been scrubbed up. This lot could talk in
sentences, about things that weren't totally football related. I
can't be entirely sure, but I think one of the patrons was
actually drinking red wine, from a glass!
John once again tried to flog a couple of our books, but the
people in the bar were more interested in discussing the social
and ethical concepts raised by our writings than actually
buying it. What is wrong with these people?
John; Tarbert has a lovely harbour in a beautiful setting and
we enjoyed drinking in its beauty before diving into 'The
Corner House' and drinking in its bevy. It was a nice pub and
the pints were excellent. We were getting very settled there but
Craig overruled Tam and I by insisting we visited another pub
as this was the reason for the trip. The fact that we were in the
wrong town did not influence him at all.

The bar staff were very friendly and the barman was very helpful, he even told us what pubs to visit. Obviously wanting rid of us, but he hid it well. **Barman rating;**
So we wandered out into the scenic grandeur again and along the front, up a wee side street and into a pub Craig claimed he knew. It was called *'The Back Bar'* and is part of The Tarbert Hotel, but was called *'The Back Bar'*, I assumed, because it was up a back street. Amazing how they make up the name for pubs. The last one, by the way, was on a corner. Work it out for yourselves.

This bar was very modern inside, all marble tiles and dark wood. Not our cup of tea, or pint. We had a good chat with the barmaid and explained what we were doing. We even let her look at a copy of our book, but she showed no interest. No class at all.

Barmaid Rating;

It was time to go and as we were all hungry (suffering from the munchies) I volunteered to nip in to the chippy, get three bags of chips and catch up with them. The chips took forever and I ended up having to rush along the front to catch up. Lucky I am quite athletic!

Craig; We needed something to eat before going back aboard the Waverley. Since time was short we decided a quick trip to the 'chippy' was in order. John volunteered to stay behind to wait for our chips while Tam and I carried on towards the pier. The man is selfless!

Like all the other cafés the chippy in Tarbert had been doing a roaring trade courtesy of the unexpected visit from our boat. The shop owners must have been clapping their hands, if not rubbing them, when The Waverley appeared on the horizon.

That's when the conspiracy theory started. Someone, I don't know who, suggested it might be similar to what happens when bus drivers visit particular service stations on the motorway. The driver gets to eat for free if he brings in a full bus load of passengers. Personally I don't see the captain of the Waverley being bought off with a deep fried pizza and a couple of pickled eggs.

I was practising my speech to explain why we had sailed away without John when he appeared, scurrying along the road. It was a close call. Part of me was a little disappointed as it was a really good speech.

Shanghaied to Tarbert and now plotting a minor mutiny against Captain Fearty

Back in Largs we managed a quick pint in Charlie Smith's then caught our train. At that time of night the ticket office was closed so we sat on the train waiting for the conductor to come round. He didn't. We took this as a sign, we were on a winner.
John; We sat up the back of the boat. The sun was still shining as we ate our chips and enjoyed a can, doesn't get much better

139

than this. Only disappointment was that nobody missed the boat, or even had to rush. Can't get everything I suppose.

On the way back to Largs, we sailed between the two Cumbrae Islands and right past Millport, where Craig's Irene was on holiday for a week. Craig is going to join her for one day. He says he doesn't like Millport like Irene, but I know he just likes a few days of freedom.

He phoned her and she said she could see the Waverley and was on the front waving a tea towel. We told her we could see her, we couldn't, but I'm sure she was pleased. The sun was still shining although Kate had just text'd me to say it was pouring all over the place with thunder and lighting. The Waverley was the place to be.

Waverly Barmen Ratings; ▨▨▨▨

We were getting off at Largs as the Waverley didn't get back to Glasgow till after 10.30pm, and where it stops is not a good place to be stuck at that time of night. We had checked the time of the trains and we had about an hour to spare, so with a heavy heart, but light wallet, we said goodbye to the Waverley and headed straight across the road into '*Charlie Smith's*', a bar we have been in and reviewed before. We enjoyed a pint there and then wandered up the street and on to the train.

The journey back to Glasgow was very pleasant, but we had to get off at Paisley Gilmour Street because of work being done on the lines, or something they do regularly on Sundays to annoy the passengers. We were told buses were laid on to take us into Glasgow. They were, as long as you didn't mind waiting half an hour. What a shambles. We had a chat with some other people and ended up sharing a taxi with a bloke, who ended up saying he had no change. So we paid the whole fare, but as we hadn't bought tickets on the train it ended up a good deal.

Craig; Unfortunately, because of line maintenance the train only took us as far as Paisley. The rest of the journey to

Away for a Wee Paddle

Glasgow was to be made on a bus provided by Scotrail, These people sometimes find it hard enough to keep the trains running. Why they would imagine themselves capable of organising buses as well is a mystery. The bus was a no show. We got a taxi from Paisley. What I didn't know was that we had an extra body in the cab along with us. My neck was giving me a lot of trouble at that point and I couldn't actually turn my head to see who was there, even if I'd known there was someone else in the car.

At first I thought John was attempting to do an impersonation of someone I'd never heard of. Either that or he was just pish at it.

As you might imagine I was a bit disorientated when I got out of the taxi to see this total stranger get out of the back seat. Just for a second I couldn't make up my mind which one of us was in the wrong taxi. It was him, I'm fairly certain.

We decided to try a new pub before getting our trains home. The one we chose was called 'Rhoderick Dhu' It was a good pub and handy for the station too. We had a nice drink while John entertained us with some of his more colourful political theories. I don't think Tam could believe what he was hearing. The world according to John can be a scary place.

We saw Tam onto his train, had another drink and went home. Or so the story goes.

Our day out had started well, and then had gradually gone downhill. Perhaps if we had checked, and believed, the weather forecast it would have been a very different story. Still, a wee sail on the Waverley is always a good day out, even if you never ever, get to your intended destination. Actually I don't know why I was surprised that the Waverley didn't reach its intended destination. A few years ago John and I were taking a wee trip on the Waverley to visit Port Ellen on Islay. Needless to say I still haven't set eyes on Port Ellen. Once again bad weather was blamed.

Away for a Wee Paddle

When planning this latest trip we were annoyed that the Sunday bus service meant that travelling to Campbeltown by bus and returning on the Waverley was too problematic. After we got home we were counting our blessings that we hadn't managed to do it.

If we had arrived in Campbeltown by bus we would have to wait another year to have a chance to complete the journey.

Assuming that someone on the Waverley knows the way there!

John; The taxi dropped us off opposite the Central Station and, for a change from *'The Horseshoe',* our regular haunt, we wandered round the corner into *'The Rhoderick Dhu'.* This is a great bar and one I've been in several times. We had a great discussion about how to cure the countries money problems, but my ultra-right wing ideas were thrown out by Craig and Tam, although I am sure the death penalty for dropping litter was taken out of context.

I asked the barman what he thought and he definitely was on Craig and Tams' side. Think I'll have to stop reading 'The Daily Mail'.

Barman Rating; 🍺🍺 (for not agreeing with me)

Finishing our pints and discussion, we wandered over to the Central Station, said goodnight to Tam, who was getting a different train, and discovered we still had half an hour till our train. I know it sounds ridiculous, but we felt we had to have another pint. So we did.

As usual, the train home was a bit of a blur, but I did manage to phone a taxi which took us the last bit home.

Craig's last words to me before we said goodbye was that he was not going to be beaten and was getting the bus to Campbeltown tomorrow. I told him he was on his own. The amazing thing is that when I got home, about 11.30pm, Kate was still up and thought I was fairly sober. Must be the sea air, or was she pissed herself. I have no idea, but I was pleased as I got up the next day feeling great, magic.

In Summary

This little adventure generated a bar staff average score of three. But that doesn't really tell the whole story of our day at sea.

The fact that we never came within thirty miles of our intended destination certainly coloured our opinion of the trip.

The ship might be ocean going but it would seem that its crew aren't. Maybe none of them can swim, hence their reluctance to go out of their depth.

We did enjoy sailing on the Waverley, who wouldn't? But it would have been nice to set foot in Campbeltown. After all we had been planning this journey, on and off, for the best part of a year.

That being said, Tarbert is still well worth a visit. It has many guesthouses, B&Bs and hotels. There is a frequent ferry service over to Portavadie and it's just 30 miles by road to Campbeltown.

The occasional visit by wayward ocean going paddle steamers also adds to the fun to be had by visitors to the town.

The only thing we really had against Tarbert was that it wasn't Campbeltown.

It was good to have Tam with us on this adventure even if he was a wee bit traumatised by the constant arguing of his two shipmates.

Stoned in the Granite City

(The northern lights of old Aberdeen
Where singers and fighters are quite often seen.)

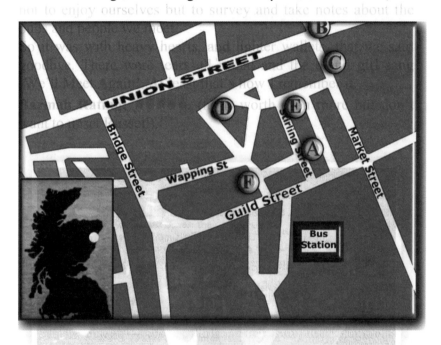

A:- The Spirit Level: **B:-** The Frigate: **C:-** Wilson's:
D:- The Old King's High: **E:-** The Market Arms:
F:- Aitchies Ale House.

East Kilbride-Glasgow-Aberdeen
Glasgow-east Kilbride
Two Buses (Golden ones)

John; We had a letter from a publisher saying our first attempt at a book was great but they thought it would have more appeal if it covered more of Scotland.

Although Craig and I are not the best at taking advice, especially Craig, we decided to take it and so we planned a trip to Aberdeen, and glad we are that we did.

I booked us on the City Link Golden Coach service. I had been on this service before to Inverness with Kate to visit my brother who has a Bed and Breakfast there, but Craig had never been on the Gold Coach before.

This is a magic service. Not only is it free (apart from 50p if you book in advance), but it is a non-stop service, you get a cup of tea, a scone or a sandwich, a bit of shortbread, and it's all free. I have no idea how much our daft parliament are throwing away on this, but it's great that they are. From now on I am voting SNP. Who cares if there's no money left for the next generation-it's great for us golden oldies.

It was an early start. Kate set the alarm for 6.45am and I had to make my own breakfast and pieces while Kate was sound asleep upstairs. I think the novelty of making my Corned Beef with English Mustard on Plain Bread pieces is wearing off. Who can blame her-I can.

Anyway, I wandered down the hill and got to Craig's house at 7.25am. It was a lovely day. Irene, (Craig's better half) answered the door and complained that it was terrible that they (meaning Kate and her) had to get up this early to see their men out. I had to tell her that Kate was in her kip and had no idea where I was or even if my pieces were up to standard. Think I am letting Kate off too lightly, I'll have to have a word with her-Aye right.

So it was the couple of steps down the hill and on to the No. 18 bus which took us right to Buchanan Street Bus Station, although there was a bit of a panic on the bus when it went a different route than normal. We thought for a minute it was not going to go to the bus station, so Craig started blaming me right away. Think he got out the bed on the wrong side this morning.

Craig; We haven't really had much to do with the east coast so far in our travels. The most easterly we have managed, if you don't count Edinburgh, and I don't, is Perth.

Despite being warned against going to Aberdeen, by an Aberdonian, no less, we decided it would be an interesting destination. It was just about as far away as we can manage without an overnight stay.

The Gold bus seemed to be the answer to our problems. Initially we intended to get the train back from Aberdeen rather than the return bus. This idea was shot down in flames by Scotrail.

When we checked the fares a week before our trip it came in at about £10 per person. Unfortunately we couldn't book it straight away and by the time John did go on to the net to book, the price had gone up to over £20 per person, sheer profiteering if you ask me.

Needless to say we turned down the opportunity to enrich Scotrail's shareholders and opted for the free bus instead.

Actually that made our travel arrangements much easier.

I had convinced John that we should get the number 18 bus into Glasgow a little earlier than we originally planned because I was certain the Gold bus would be very busy and we might have trouble getting two seats together. The memory of our trip to Glencoe still haunts me. I'll never forget all the old buggers pushing their way onto the bus and then each taking a window seat. That wasn't going to happen this time.

Things didn't start too well it has to be said. The driver of the number 18 had his own agenda. I doubt if he got the bus over 15 mph at any point in the journey. I don't know if he was just afraid of speed or he was just the crappiest driver in the depot.

Add to that the road works and one serious diversion and you can almost smell the frustration we felt. Against all the odds we did make it on time and to celebrate I suggested we go into the shop in the bus station. You would think we would know better by now.

John; After getting our papers and a bottle of coke and a bottle of water (I had a thirst from a day out in Glasgow yesterday), we wandered over to the stance where we could see the Golden Bus, it is actually painted Gold. All they need to do is put the Golden Coach sign in Gaelic to keep Scotland's two teuchters' happy.

Craig panicked when we saw that people were already getting on the bus, so we were last on, but the bus was only half full (or in Craig's mood, half empty), so we could pick our seat. We had worked out which side we would sit on to keep out of the sun. How often do you have to worry about that in Scotland?

When he saw how luxurious the bus was, Craig cheered up and admitted it was a really great. There was a toilet and everything.

At 9.00am the bus left and we enjoyed a great run up to Aberdeen. We got our scones, tea and shortbread, all free. We had a laugh when the bus went over a few bumps on the road. The problem was that our cups of tea were firmly positioned in the wee holes on the trays that folded down. The tea started bouncing about and went everywhere. It wouldn't have been so funny if a wee women opposite us hadn't started really knotting herself, she couldn't stop. It was hysterical. After she settled down and went to the toilet to change her knickers, she started talking to us, whether we wanted her to or not.

She is a member of a group called 'Still Dancing'. She told us all about it, and how a guy from Govan had left when he was 22 and has been all over the world dancing. Didn't sound like anyone I knew from Govan, and I've been all over the world drinking.

I've forgotten what the bloke from Govan has got to do with the old biddies dancing, but it was a good story.

After going through some thick fog, we went over a river, I think it would have been 'The Dee', but might have been 'The Don', bit sad that I don't really care. Anyway, we arrived in Aberdeen Bus Station in glorious sunshine and got off the bus to start our discovery of 'The Granite City'.

Craig; We bought papers, juice and mints for the journey. It was only when we came out did we realise our bus was in, and it was loading. How we managed to miss spotting a huge gold painted bus I'll never know. After all my careful planning we ended up last in the queue, and I was far from happy. As it turned out there were plenty of seats.

I was very impressed with the Gold bus. It was a very smoothly run and comfortable service. We decided there and then that this service was just too good to share with anyone. I told John that when we got back we had to tell everybody that the service was substandard and downright manky. If word ever gets out about just how good it really was the bus will be infested with octogenarian day trippers.

We arrived in Aberdeen at about 11.40am and the sun was shining. In fact it was so hot that I suggested we should take shelter from the harmful rays of the sun in a nearby pub. John immediately saw the wisdom of this action and we headed for the 'Spirit Level'.

John; Craig had, as usual, been on to Google to find where the pubs are, and there were plenty within a short distance of the Bus Station.

The first pub we went into was called *'The Spirit Level'*, this would be just before 12.00 noon and there were a few regulars in, and they were all pissed, especially one wee guy who right away started talking to us. I was worried that we would not understand what Aberdonians were saying because of their accent being completely different from our West of Scotland one. This turned out not to be a problem as almost all the people we met in the pubs we went into came from other parts of Scotland, and had moved to Aberdeen for work, or other reasons.

The wee guy who started talking was the most pissed. He said he'd been in Aberdeen for 34 years, I think. After finding out where we came from, his first question was what foot do you kick with. I've never heard that question for years and because unlike Glasgow, where you have a fair idea who kicks with what foot by the pub your in, I had no idea who he supported, so didn't know what to say so as not to offend him, although I was not bothered because Craig, the hardest man in Auchinleck, was beside me.

Suzanne manages to keep smiling, despite the karaoke.

149

Stoned in the Granite City

Although I no longer have any interest in football, I told the truth and said I used to support Rangers when I was a boy. He said that although he had been up here for over 30 years, he was the happiest Celtic man on the planet. I don't think he knew what planet he was on. He said it was no problem, I think Craig growled at him.

The juke box, or whatever they call it now, was on, and all the guys were joining in the singing, it was amazing. They were harmonizing and were fantastic. It was like the X factor only the singers were great.

We got talking to the barmaid, a lovely girl called Suzanne, who explained that the reason they were all pissed was that the pub opened at 7 o'clock in the morning. What a place Aberdeen is. I was starting to like it. The funny thing is that Suzanne told us that the wee pissed guy was self-employed as a painter and decorator. I was certain he would be a plasterer! He is seemingly very good, but as soon as he finishes a job, he just drinks the money. Nothing wrong with that I say.

We told Suzanne about the book we had written and what we were doing in Aberdeen. Thank God it was early in the day because I had no idea what we were doing by the time we left. She agreed to have her photo taken with Craig if we mentioned her in our next book. After a couple of pints, one more than we had agreed to, we felt we had to go if we wanted to visit all the pubs Craig had planned. So it was with fond farewells' and with the sound of the guys singing 'The Northern Lights', we exited the 'Spirit Level'.

Barmaid Score; ▓▓▓▓▓, (Suzanne was really great)

Craig; As soon as we entered the place we knew we had made the right decision. It was a great pub. We did however think it was a bit strange to find so many people enjoying a tipple at that time of the day, but decided to put it down to the east coast air. Usually our first pub of the day has only intrepid pub reviewers and the odd enthusiastic amateur as customers.

Stoned in the Granite City

The customers nearest the bar were particularly friendly, and loud. It turns out they were both originally from Glasgow and wanted to talk about it. To listen to them you would think we were on the other side of the world, not three hours up the road. Of course the vast amount of booze they were sloshing down their throats might tend to bring on a bout of nostalgia. The two of them started singing along with the juke box, after a fashion. One of them kept getting the words mixed up. His pal seemed to think he was doing it on purpose, just to annoy him. This led to great argument and, to us meek mannered sowels, looked as if it might come to blows. As quick as it flared up the row would end in handshakes and cuddles. They would be the best of friends again, until the next chorus. In other words, it was a pretty standard example of Scottish pub banter.

The barmaid, Suzanne, told us that these two gentlemen, formerly of the Govan area in Glasgow, had been hard at it since seven o'clock that morning. That went a long way towards explaining their present condition. I really wanted to take a picture of the pair of them but settled on taking one of Suzanne instead as she didn't look quite so homicidal.

We were enjoying ourselves so much that we decided to make the 'Spirit Level' a two pint stop. The barmaid seemed quite interested in our wee adventures and suggested another bar which could be of interest to us. She said that we might be in for a very pleasant surprise if we visited it. Being just a tad paranoid I assumed that she was just trying to get rid of us, but she was spot on

John; We followed Suzanne's instructions and wandered into *'The Clipper'*, which she told us was a great pub.

Craig bolted up the stairs to the toilet and left me to order the pints. I was holding the kitty. The woman behind the bar, who again did not have an Aberdeen accent, asked me if I was a pensioner. I thought she was being cheeky, as I am sure I look much younger than my 64 years, but it turns out that old guys

151

like me get 45 pence off the price of a pint. This was turning out to be some day. Craig came back just as she was telling me this and let her know that he was a pensioner too. He would say anything to get a cheap pint. We were as happy as Larry. We spoke to this angel for a wee while and drank our cheap booze. Craig was all for staying here all day when the barmaid told us that cheap drink for the oldies was normal in many pubs, this was getting better and better. She told us about a pub called *'Jimmy Wilson's'*, where her sister-in-law works, which also does the cheap drink. So following her instructions, we wandered off in the sunshine to find it.

Barmaid Score; ▮▮▮▮, one less than Suzanne, but still good. The pub was called *'Wilson's*, not *'Jimmy Wilson's'*, and it said it was a Sports Bar, so I was sure it couldn't be the one she was talking about, but after a bit of wandering about and asking more Aberdonians, who sounded nothing like Aberdonians, we wandered into the bar.

Inside was nothing like what a traditional sports bar is supposed to. It had photos of football stars and strips on the walls, but none of the big tellies you normally get in a sports bar. We asked the woman behind the bar if she was the sister-in-law of the lady in the Clipper, and she admitted she was and guessed we wanted the cheap drink. She was right.

The pints were fine but the place was not as good as the first two pubs and the woman behind the bar ignored us. It was just like being back in the West. However, cheap pints are cheap pints, but we had no information about other pubs which do the same so we just had to hope for the best.

Barmaid Score; ▮▮; getting gradually worse

Craig; 'The Frigate' was only a ten minute stroll away, she told us. Just outside the 'Spirit Level' we met an older bloke who was having a quiet smoke. He also said 'The Frigate' was a good 'man's pub'.

Stoned in the Granite City

We had no difficulty finding it, even though it was on a back street at the entrance to a tunnel. I had to make a quick toilet stop so John went into the bar to order up the beer. The stairs up to the toilet were really interesting. They actually looked like they belonged on an old sailing ship. Unfortunately the toilet itself looked like it belonged in a derelict tenement.

We were both smiling from ear to ear when we found out that we 'qualified' for a cheap pint. That is the kind of surprise I really like, even if it means pretending to be a pensioner. Actually I would have been better pleased if the barmaid had queried my age, just a wee bit. I then noticed the old boy I had been talking to down at 'The Spirit'. He was standing behind us. John, ever the diplomat, asked him if he was stalking us. It turned out he was doing his usual rounds of his favorite pubs.

He told us about another pub and said it was really good and cheap. I'm really getting a bit worried about our image. Everyone seems to think we are a bit careful with our pennies.

Anyway, I think our newest pal must have started out at the same time as those two nutters in our first pub, because he was quite obviously talking mince. Wilson's was rotten. The barmaid was either having a very bad day or she was on the downward swing in a cycle of depression. She certainly didn't seem to take to us anyway. The pub was supposedly a 'Sports Bar' but since I was the youngest person in the place, you've got to ask just what sort of sports are on offer. I would imagine whippet racing and champion's league dominos are rarely off the television.

John; As we were getting hungry, we decided to wander up to Union Street and see if there was a bit of greenery where we could sit down and have our pieces. After a wee walk in the sunshine we found a nice park and sat in the shade to have our picnic. Because I had made my own, I only had pieces, whereas Craig had bits of chicken, chocolate biscuits and everything. Kate's getting out her bed for our next trip, if she feels like it.

Craig had a couple of Blue Ribband chocolate biscuits, which are magic. He must have felt sorry for me and gave one to me. As I was eating it, he broke his and half of it fell on the path. What a laugh. Craig would never pick up food that had fallen on the ground, so I did and ended up with one and a half biscuits, Craig only had a half. I thought this was really funny, Craig didn't laugh.

John takes steps to make sure we don't go thirsty.

After we finished our lunch, which was great, we wandered about and found a nice looking pub called *'The Old King's High'*. It was not as atmospheric as we like and it was very expensive. Even after we mentioned how old we were, there was no discount. The barman was quiet and kept himself to himself. This is more like what I thought Aberdeen might have been, but up to now is not. But it is a really friendly place, so we still enjoyed our pints.

Barman Score; ▮▮.

Craig; One pint was enough for us and then we moved on. We found a nice wee park to have our picnic lunch. It was called Union Terrace Gardens, just off Union Street. John seemed less than pleased with his food. I knew this because he harped on about it at great length. I decided to save myself some major ear ache and donated some of my lavish supplies to him.

My theory was, if he is eating, he isn't talking. It was only a partial success. After lunch we took a few photos of Union Street just to prove we'd been there, then moved on to the real work of the day.

'The Old Kings High' was quite a good, if strangely named pub. I would have asked the barmaid to explain the pubs weird name but she didn't strike me as the helpful sort so I left it a mystery. There was some sort of music quiz on one of the pubs televisions and we joined in with the friendly customers.

I decided to ingratiate myself with them by getting every single question wrong. They seemed to appreciate my efforts and there was a lot of friendly banter and laughter.

John; We left the pub and wandered down towards the docks area and into *'The Market Arms'*. This pub is, without doubt, the scariest pub with the hardest people we have ever been in outside Port Glasgow or Saltcoats. Having said that, we liked it and had a great time talking to the barman who was obviously employed because of his ability to scare the shit out of anyone. He was a great bloke.

By the time we had got our pints there was a fight going on between a man and a woman, fisty cuffs and everything, what a laugh. Don't want to say much more about the place 'cause I'd like to come back to Aberdeen which is a great place, especially the cheap drink.

So we finished our drinks, went outside, stepped over the body of the man and buggered off sharply to look for another, possibly quieter pub.

Barman Score; ▓▓▓▓▓ (shit scared to give him less)

After wandering, or staggering along the road, we found a pub called '*Aitchies Ale House*'. This was the complete opposite of '*The Market Arms*'. It was very posh with two old gentlemen behind the bar in white shirts and black trousers. How I remember this after god knows how many pints I don't know, but it is encouraging I have still some memory left.

Although this was a nice pub, and very safe, it lacked any fun and after a pint and a chat with the barmen, who were shocked about us being in the previous bar, we decided it was time to head back to the bus station and find our Golden bus.

Barmen Score; ▓▓▓▓; (mainly for smart dress sense)

Craig; We headed back in the general direction of the bus station knowing there were a few pubs nearby. Unfortunately for us, I spotted one called 'The Market Arms' and insisted we go in. John wasn't keen but I convinced him it would be good to see the less fortunate at play. What an eye opener!

From the outside it looked a bit run down and neglected. It was no surprise to find that this theme continued on the inside, and not just the décor. While waiting for our beers we wondered how appropriate the pub's name, 'Market Arms' was, and what might be a better name for it. I thought it might attract more of the right sort of crowd if they changed the name to 'The Bottom of the Barrel'. John suggested something like 'The Soap Dodger's Lounge'.

We were still sniggering like a pair of schoolboys when the drama began. A young scary women came screaming into the bar. It wasn't the blood streaming down her face that made her scary. It was just her face. She had one of these clock-stoppingly gaunt faces which are just frightening. If you turned round suddenly and saw it you couldn't stop yourself from flinching.

I couldn't make out a word she was saying. This might have been because she was either drunk, on drugs or just crazy. It's also quite possible all three conditions were working on the poor lassie at the same time. Anyway, the barman seemed to know what was going on and in a practiced move leapt over the bar and sprinted out of the front door.

Two things happened simultaneously at this point. The sound level outside increased greatly, while inside the level of our beer went down extremely quickly.

**We get ringside seats at the Market Arms,
and it is a pints decision.**

By the time we had finished our drinks the barman was back behind the bar, working away as if nothing unusual had happened. In this place that was probably true. The young

157

woman's blood stained face was being sponged down by a couple of her friends, and the rest of the customers, or denizens, as I was now calling them, just continued with whatever it was they were doing before all of the melee kicked off.

I fully expected to find the chalk outline of a body on the pavement outside 'The Market Arms' as we left. To be honest there might have been one but, we were going so fast it would have been easy to miss it.

John; We bought sandwiches and drinks for the bus. Alcohol and hot food are not allowed, aye right! I had a laugh before getting on the bus. There was a queue, but there were two buses, and as we were not sure if the queue was for the Gold bus or the other one, which was also going to Glasgow, I went up to a wee women at the front of the queue and asked her if this was the front of the queue. She said it was so I stood beside her. There were a lot of murmurs from behind, so I went to the back and joined Craig, who is no fun, or just not as drunk as I was.

The journey back to Glasgow was lovely. Craig had checked out the seating on the way up to Aberdeen and found that there were a couple of seats near the back that were at the emergency exit and had loads of legroom, and were also near the toilet. So we sat there and enjoyed the sunset as we headed for Glasgow.

The idea was that when we got off the bus we would head into *'The Horshoe'*, our usual watering hole on our way home through Glasgow, but it was so packed we couldn't even get in the door. I think there must have been a football match on or something. Anyway, we decided that since there was a train due in a few minutes, we would get it and be back in EK in time for a couple of pints in *'The Monty'*. As usual the train was packed. Why they put on trains to EK with only two coaches is beyond me. EK is a big place for goodness sake. We had to stand for the first couple of stations. We got a seat eventually and nodded off on the way home.

Revitalized, we got off the train and enjoyed a couple of pints in *'The Monty'* before being collected by Irene and taken home.

The trip to Aberdeen was great. It was much nicer than I remembered from being there years ago and the pubs, at least most of them were great, and cheap. The only thing is I don't remember talking to anyone with an Aberdeenshire accent. Fitlike the noo.

Craig; *I noticed John was looking a little bit white and shaken. There was only one course of action, a stiff drink. We had left The Market at such a rate of knots that we didn't notice which direction we were taking. It was sheer good luck that we managed to find 'Aitchies Ale House'. I think we deserved some good luck after the trauma of 'The Market Arms'.*

'Aitchies Ale House' didn't look like the kind of place that had ever seen any trouble. It certainly didn't have any jakies hanging about the place.

The old boys behind the bar looked as if the pub had been built around them, many years ago. They seemed genuinely stunned when we told them we had been in the Market. I took this to mean that they knew quality when they saw it and knew we didn't belong in a place like that. John saw it differently. He was convinced that they were amazed two West Coast wimps like us had survived a visit to that hell hole.

It was a good pint but very expensive. It left me wondering if these two 'auld yins' were topping up their pension plans with the extra cash. Our time in Aberdeen was up so we made our way back to the bus station, stopping only for a few essentials for the journey home.

The journey fairly flashed by. There may have been some power napping involved. We were wide awake by the time our great bus reached the outskirts of Glasgow and were looking forward to a beer or two in 'The Horse Shoe'.

I could tell that the pub was far too busy even before we got to the door. The noise was tremendous, but not in the good sense of the word. There was no way we could get into the bar, never mind get a pint. We couldn't understand why there was such a crowd. I had an uneasy feeling that Tennant's were having a lager promotion in the pub and we hadn't been invited. Now that would be ironic as we had just travelled a couple of hundred miles to the home of the most expensive pint I've ever had.

Ever adaptable, we decided to hold off on the booze until we got to EK. 'The Monty' was once again our last port of call. Two pints of lager later we were on our way home curtsey of Irene.

It had been a great day out. I have to admit I hadn't been sure of what we could expect this particular trip. Aberdeen has never been one of my favourite places. Actually I'd only been there three times before and I hadn't really enjoyed the experience very much.

This time had been different. We had met quite a few people on our journey and for the most part they had been very friendly and helpful. The pubs, with one glaring exception, had been great and the bus service had been unbelievably good. I would thoroughly recommend a visit to the city and of course The Golden Bus. Actually don't tell anyone about bus OK!

In Summary

The high point of of this trip was not the pubs, the friendly people or even the scenery. No the highlight of our day out in old Aberdeen was the transport to and from it.

The Gold Bus was amazing. Why can't all buses be like this? It's almost worth the long trip just to travel on this bus.

The only downside is that on the Gold Bus, or any other bus for that matter, is you cannot get a wee drink, a real drink. As we've said before, our Scottish Parliament know how to put a damper on a good outing.

We didn't know what we were getting ourselves into when Aberdeen was chosen for our day out. The city doesn't always come out top of the league for friendliness, if you're to believe all the nonsense you hear in Lowland pubs.

However we did enjoy our short stay there, finding a couple of really good pubs. What impressed us most was the scheme which some of the pubs run where the over 60s get a hefty price reduction on the booze of their choice. Let all other pubs take note.

There were one or two dodgy moments during our tour, but that's not peculiar to Aberdeen. We could easily have avoided them if we had wanted to, but we are far too nosey for that. It's a tough life, that of the part-time pub reviewer.

Aberdeen scored an impressive 3.66 average on our highly suspect scale of good bar service, placing it in second place overall.

Glasgow, Goin Roon an Roon
(The only trouble wi Glasgow is ye leave the pubs too soon)

EK-Bridgeton-Parkhead-The Barrows-Maryhill
Byres Road-Partick-Linthouse-Govan-Glasgow-EK

162

Glasgow, Goin Roon an Roon

John; We had talked about a trip like this for a while, but I think Craig was a bit afraid to venture into some of the areas concerned, like them all. But these are the real places where people who worked in Glasgow lived, before East Kilbride and places like it were invented. Nowadays they are full of people who, in many cases through no fault of their own, are unemployed. A bit sad really.

These areas are also full of really hard men, and harder women, and you've got to watch what you say in many of the pubs, especially in Bridgeton and Parkhead.

Up until the day before this trip, we had planned to go on a completely different trip, taking in places like Balmaha, Luss and Balloch. The trip also included a ferry trip from Balmaha to Luss. Now Craig, as some of you will know, has a bad track record when it comes to ferry trips being cancelled or changed at the last minute due to bad weather, or in the case of the Waverley, if the captain even feels he has wind.

So the day before Craig had a look at the forecast which predicted wind and some rain. This is the West of Scotland, what did he expect, a heat-wave! But he would not be put off, so we played safe and did the inland trip with no ferries to worry about. Needless to say it was a scorcher, but by the time we realized Craig's forecast was out the window, it was too late to do the original trip.

So with Craig praying for rain, we got on our first bus, the 18, at about 10.30am to take us to Bridgeton Cross, where we alighted in brilliant sunshine, which made the Union Jacks and the red, white and blue paintwork, which adorned almost every building, look very nice indeed, in a proddy sort of way.

Craig; Our original intention was to have a leisurely and scenic trip to and across Loch Lomond. The actual trip we took was far from scenic and by no stretch of the imagination could it be described as leisurely.

Glasgow, Goin Roon an Roon

John had been looking forward to sailing across the loch for some time and had put a lot of effort into the planning of the trip. He was keen to complete this journey before the end of the summer as we don't know if the ferry service continues into September.

We met in the pub the night before the Trip and John produced his master plan. There were pages upon pages of computer print outs, detailing every aspect of the proposed day out. He had allowed time for refreshment stops, with options to extend individual breaks, in case we were really enjoying the scenic grandeur and or the beer.

It was all very neat and professional looking. What a pity it wasn't used. I almost feel guilty about what happened. The fact is I had been watching the weather forecast and it didn't look too good.

Loch Lomond is set in one of the most beautiful areas of Scotland and is a major tourist attraction. The problem with fantastic scenery is, that to truly appreciate it you have to be able to see it in the first place. On a rainy, misty August morning Loch Lomond, or any other large body of water for that matter, can be a miserable place to be. I suggested that we should play it safe and think about changing our destination.

Unfortunately, John took this to mean that I wanted to do what he called the 'Outer Circle' of pubs in Glasgow. I didn't, but by the time he had finished going on about it I didn't have the nerve to veto this plan as well.

On the morning of the trip I was panicking a bit at the prospect of journeying into the bad lands of Glasgow. In a desperate bid to avoid this I came up with a plan B. As the weather wasn't behaving as predicted, in fact it was what you might call fine sailing weather, I decided that it would be a great idea to rejig the original Loch Lomond trip. With only a few minutes to spare before John arrived at my place I managed to scribble down a new timetable onto a piece of scrap paper. I handed it to him at the bus stop. When you consider how much effort he had put into his plan it's hardly surprising that he didn't appear to be overly impressed. In fact, for the first time in a very long time, he was rendered speechless. As you can imagine this state of affairs didn't last very long. After listening to a couple of minutes worth of ranting I gave in and agreed to the Glasgow trip.

Although I lived in Glasgow for a couple of years I don't really know many areas in the city, except of course by reputation. If you fancy a wee drink on the south side or the city centre I'm your man, but anywhere else I'd be a bit lost.

With that in mind I handed over all responsibility for planning our route to John. To be honest after talking him out of his trip to Loch Lomond I had decided to keep a low profile on any decision making.

John; Bridgeton Cross, or Brigton to the locals, has had a lot of improvements done in the last few years, and the statue sort of structure in the centre of the wee roundabout has been freshly painted (no need to tell you the colours).

We wandered up and down the street looking at the various pubs and admiring the flags outside them. After a few minutes to allow the smell of bleach to subside, we wandered into '*Walkers*'. The pub was spotless, the pints were great and the barman was friendly, all in all a great place for a morning pint. It has to be said that if the fact that the walls are covered with photographs of Rangers players, Ibrox, the Queen and other members of the Royal Family bothers you, then this is not the pub for you. But apart from that minor point, the pub was great.

As we were leaving I noticed the barman was having, what looked like a meeting with about half a dozen young women. I would have loved to find out what it was about, but didn't like to ask. I was too frightened (of the women). Brigton in general looked great in the sunshine, which was annoying Craig. To be fair, I kept talking about how lovely Loch Lomond would be looking in the sunshine.

Barman Rating;

Keeping the flag flying in Bridgeton.

Craig; Given Glasgow's much publicised religious divide I had opted for neutral colours when getting dressed for this journey. John, possibly still in a bit of a huff at not getting a wee shot on a boat, decided to dress himself from head to toe in bright blue. That's what I call a master stroke in forward planning. I was going to be the guy strolling along beside the slow moving target.

Bridgeton was our first stop of the day. At least here John, the master of disguise, wouldn't stick out like a sore thumb. This little slice of Glasgow is very definitely blue. We paced up and down at the cross looking for a non-threatening pub to start our day in. No easy task! Eventually we settled on 'Walker's'.

Glasgow, Goin Roon an Roon

It looked like a traditional, old fashioned, man's pub. The outside would have been very drab looking but the Union Jacks flying in the wind above the doors fairly brightened the place up.

It took us a few moments to decide which entrance to go in. We assumed that one would lead into the bar and the other into the lounge. Wrong, they both led into the bar. It really was an old style pub with a high square bar filling up most of the space. It fairly took me back to the early 70s and my happy memories of underage drinking in Dick's hotel in Auchinleck.

We sat at a small table enjoying our reasonably priced pints and admiring the many, many photographs of the royal family which hung on every wall.

At that time of the morning, just after 11am, it was very quiet in the bar. To create a bit of an atmosphere John thought we should play some music on the juke box. I pointed out that, given where we were, the machine was probably packed with a hundred different versions of the national anthem. We decided to drink in silence.

John; We waited about 10 minutes for our next bus to take us along to Parkhead. While we waited for the bus, the locals who were waiting with us all seemed very nice and friendly. One of the guys waiting was wearing a bright purple top with a cross round his neck. That guy had no fear, or was just plain daft. Mind you, I was wearing my royal blue rain jacket and we were heading for Parkhead. I'm just daft.

While we were on the bus it started raining, quite heavily. This fairly cheered up Craig, who reckoned that at the time the rain started, we would have been in the middle of Loch Lomond getting soaked. What a man.

We got off at Parkhead Cross, or I think that's what it's called and as it was raining heavily, I put up my royal blue hood. I stood out like a sore thumb.

We had a quick look at the new buildings going up for the Commonwealth Games. They looked impressive, in a what a complete waste of money sort of a way.

We had to duck under scaffolding to get into the pub on the corner called *'The London Tavern'*, which was shut, although the door was open. The barman, who looked as if he was ready for business told us it was opening on Thursday after extensive improvements being made. Good to see the old traditional pubs managing to stay in business. He told us there was a good wee pub just across the road. So across the road we went. It was a hell of a wide road, and pouring. By the time we arrived at *'The Oak Bar'*, I was soaked. It gave me a good excuse to take off the Royal Blue jacket. Buggered if I wasn't wearing a Royal Blue shirt underneath. Don't know why I was bothering, nobody else was.

This was another nice old man's pub and again the pints were great. You definitely get better pints in pubs that rely on regulars of an age who know what a good pint is.

The pub from the outside looked pretty grim, but looks can be deceiving, it's a great wee pub.

Barman Rating; ♔♔♔♔

Craig; Outside again, we waited for the next bus which would take us to our next refreshment stop, Parkhead. I often wonder why bus companies ever bother to print timetables as they always end up as works of fiction. We waited about half an hour for a bus which was supposed to be with us within five minutes.

The delay gave John time to worry about his choice of clothing. I tried to take his mind off his impending fate by explaining that all the really psycho neds in Parkheid were probably still sleeping off their last drink fuelled 'rumble'. Strangely this didn't seem to settle him in the least.

It had started to rain by this time so that brightened up my day no end. I kept pointing at the dark clouds and reminding John that, but for me, he would now be stuck out in the middle of Loch Lomond during a raging storm.

Once we hit the pavement we decided it would be a good idea to keep moving and not look like a couple of tourists. It was either the driving rain or the speed we were careering along at that caused us to make a bit of an arse of ourselves. I thought that 'The London Tavern' was having its shutters taken down. Actually it was closed for business. We piled in the open front door and demanded two pints from a rather startled looking barman. He looked at us as if we were mad. He maybe had a point. After apologising we made our way up the road to 'The Oak Bar'.

Not much of a View up at Celtic Park.

It seemed to me that architecturally this pub might have been modelled on a World War Two bunker, it wasn't a pretty sight. Inside you would be forgiven for thinking that time had stood still, possibly since 1911 or there about. It could have been a museum piece or a stage set made for a period play. The décor depended heavily on wood cladding and had a hand built quality to it. Unfortunately those hands were not very skilled ones.

Our beer was reasonably cheap and, since we obviously were not paying a premium for our surroundings, that seemed only fair. The barmaid and the customers seemed quite friendly so we relaxed a little. Although, every time the heavy door to the bar opened John would grab his bright blue jacket and try to stuff it further down behind his bar stool.

John; By the time we wandered back outside, the rain had eased to a downpour. When we studied the timetable at the bus stop, we discovered there was a bus we could get, the number 90 that would take us all the way to Govan, which was one of the places we were going to visit later in the day. But a combination of the convoluted route it took, and that we had a planned route already agreed made us stick to the original route. Don't know why we discussed a change in the first place.

Our planned bus, I've forgotten the number, turned up and we had a nice wee run to 'The Barras' area where we got off. We both had some of our pieces, mine with Corned Beef and English mustard as usual, as we wandered around. The sun had come back out again so we had a look at The Barras, which are completely different when they are closed. They only open at the weekends. There are some great wee pubs in the area, catering for the Celtic supporters who stay in this area. One of them I think was called 'Tim Land'. What a great name for a pub, but it was shut, so we wandered about and in to a pub called 'The Old Burnt Barns'. This was a beautiful pub inside. The decorations and memorabilia were fantastic; especially the Red Indian with a Celtic scarf on, and again the beer was great. The locals were all friendly, the barmaid was good, but was wearing a Green top with a Celtic crest on it, so you were in no doubt which side of the great divide you were in. It was one of the nicest pubs we had been in and would like to have asked the history behind the unusual name of the pub, but we were sure that people in this bar should know this information and didn't want to look like we were strangers. Craig and I don't like to stand out in pubs in football fanatical areas of Glasgow.

Barmaid Rating; ♝♝♝♝ (this is the third pub in a row getting four Russells. Just shows you the old areas are the best).

A brilliant beer at a Barras boozer!

Craig; We got off the bus near to the world famous 'Barras' Actually I'm not sure just how famous they really are but Glasgow folk seem to think they are pretty well known. John claimed to know a couple of good pubs in the area. What he didn't know was that they were both shut. That's how we ended up in 'The Old Burnt Barns'. It was a fantastic pub. Well worth all that wandering around in circles looking at former licenced premises. The 'Barns' was very well decorated and spotless. It is probably the best example of an Irish pub that I've seen in years, including some I've been in over in Ireland. Even the toilets were great, a bit weird but great just the same. I would have been quite happy to end our trip and just stay in this pub for the rest of the afternoon. But John declared that it was time to move on.

We had a long way to go to get to the underground station at St. Enoch. At first we tried to get a bus but for some reason they were a bit thin on the ground, so we had to walk. About half way there John's drinking caught up with him. He needed a rest stop, and very quickly. His solution to this predicament was to visit 'Sloans'. To my mind this is a bit of a yuppie pub and not at all my kind of place. John scurried to the toilet while I ordered up the refreshments, or at least tried to. The barmaid, a uni student type, told me that there was no draught beer in the pub. If this had been a real pub with real trained bar staff, this would have told to me attached to a long explanation and heartfelt apology. Not in this place. The dizzy bugger actually expected me to settle for some 'nancy-boy' bottled beer. I hate amateurs, I really do. She looked shocked when I told her that I wouldn't bother having anything at all.

I waited at the door of the beerless pub and collected John when he eventually emerged from the toilet. Having saved ourselves at least eight quid we moved on to St. Enoch's. At the station John asked if there was such a thing as a concessionary day ticket for the underground. The look on the ticket vendor's face suggested that she had never heard such a perverted suggestion in her life. A simple no would have sufficed.

John; So we said our goodbyes, wandered out into the sunshine and all the way to Glasgow Cross, and along Argyle Street to the Subway Station in St. Enoch's Square.

On the way along Argyle Street I was bursting for the toilet and the easiest thing to do was find a Pub. So with no difficulty I talked Craig into nipping into '*Sloans*', which claims to be one of the oldest pubs in Glasgow. I bolted to the toilet leaving Craig to get the pints. When I exited the toilet, feeling great, Craig was outside the toilet door and led me straight out. I was amazed at him not wanting a pint. However he then told me that there was no draught beer at all in the pub. Bit of a shocker that.

We wandered down the moving stairs to the Subway Station and enquired if they did a reduced day ticket for old people. I thought this would be a good idea as we were going to be on about four subways during the course of the day. Amazingly to me, they do not do anything like a day ticket, so we had to pay separately for each journey. Although you get a wee discount for being old and having a bus pass, it would be sensible if you could get a cheap day pass. I would write to my MSP if I could be bothered, which I can't.

One of the things I noticed at one of the stations, I can't remember which, is that the platform is very narrow and it would be easy to fall onto the track if you were a bit unsteady on your feet, like old, or drunk people, or in our case, both.

A lot of kids nowadays go on a 'Sub Crawl', which is going round on the Subway, getting off for a pint at every station. There are 13 stations I think, so there must be a lot of kids staggering along these narrow platforms. Amazing nobody has fallen in front of a train. They probably have and just bounced off.

Craig; Maryhill was our next stop. My faith in John as expedition leader was sorely tested in Maryhill. Actually I think it's his eyesight which needs tested. He has led us into some dead end, depressing dumps in the last few years, but trying to gate-crash an undertaker's is a new low, even for him. I can't imagine what kind of trauma we would have caused, rumbling in the front door and demanding booze. It's unlikely that grieving relatives would be in the right frame of mind to see the

173

It would have been a grave error of judgement rumbling into this 'pub'.

funny side of our little drunken gaffe. Although I do have to admit that the exterior of the place did look a bit like a pub.

It was fortunate for all concerned that I managed to spot a real pub just up the road.

The Royalty Bar was a welcome, if slightly whiffy place to stop for a quick drink. I think there may be a slight problem with dampness in the bar. It took me almost three quarters of a pint of Tennent's before I could acclimatise myself to the pub's rather weird aroma. Anyway, it was a reasonable pint and it seemed like a friendly enough little bar. John claimed that the pub's great claim to fame was that it had a connection to Partick Thistle Football Club. I don't know much about football but I would have thought that this little nugget was a piece of knowledge best kept secret.

Next on our list was Oran Mor. I had heard of the pub but never visited it. Housed in an old church the Oran Mor is a very middle class establishment, where many of its customers go to see and be seen. Apparently quite a few 'Z list' Scottish celebs like to hang out in the bar drinking whatever happens to be the in drink of the day, certainly not big manly pints of beer. In fact I'm surprised they actually have pint glasses in the place at all.

I was amazed that John would want to visit this place. Maybe he thinks that as an author he should be rubbing shoulders with the great and the good of Scottish show business. That being said, he always has been a little bit star struck. I seem to remember a trip to Inveraray when he got really excited at the news that a film crew was working in the town. He couldn't have got off that bus any faster if he'd used an ejector seat.

The bar itself is very interesting and very well furnished but, the pub is, like many of its patrons, a bit of a fake. There was no banter to be had with the bar staff. Maybe we didn't meet the exacting standards required for their attention. I thought about pretending John had once played a corpse in an episode of Taggart to see if that got us any better service. One thing I was sure of was that under no circumstances were we leaving a tip. We probably couldn't afford to leave enough money to impress them anyway.

John; We got off at St. George's Cross Station and wandered up Maryhill Road. Maryhill is another great traditional area and is full of proper pubs. The first one I noticed was on a corner and looked to fit the bill. It was called T. & R. O'Brien's and I thought it might be nice to go to an Irish Bar. Just as we were crossing the road to go in I noticed it was an Undertakers. What a laugh, imagine wandering in and trying to get a couple of stiff drinks. It would be nice and quiet though.

Anyway, after looking about to make sure nobody had seen us making a fool of ourselves, we walked further up the road and went into *'The Royalty Bar'*. This bar had Union Jacks and Lion Rampart Flags outside, so we reckoned it must be the Maryhill Rangers Supporters Club, Scottish members only.

It was another nice pub inside, and catered for mainly Partick Thistle and Rangers supporters. There was a poster up on the wall giving details of The Jackie Husband Partick Thistle supporters club. Jackie was one of Thistles greatest players and worked beside my dad in Alexander Stephen's Engine Drawing Office. They were good friends. It's funny to think of a player who played for a reasonably big club (which in those days Thistle was) and also represented his country, had to work full time to manage to make a living. How times have changed. We enjoyed another good pint in good surroundings. I know this will seem strange to some people that I mention this, but there was a Black guy in the pub. In all the pubs we have visited, especially in older areas like Maryhill, it is very unusual to see a Black man having a drink. I think they have a lot more sense that their White brothers. Hope this is not a racist comment, it's not meant to be.

Barman Rating; ▓▓▓ (got to have a change-no offence barman)

As a wee aside, I was a ball boy for Thistle for a season many years ago, it was great fun. An old relative of ours, Willie Ross, was Thistle's physiotherapist for many years and treated my knee when I had cartilage trouble while playing for the great 'Govan High Former Pupils'. So I have always had a soft spot for Partick Thistle, 'The Harry Rags', 'The Maryhill Magyars', 'The Jags'.

For the last couple of years, one of my sons, Gregor, has given me a Christmas present of a ticket to one of Thistles games in January. Although it might sound like a bit of a tight fisted present, a crowd of us end up going, including Gregor, and it's always a great day. Last January we saw Thistle hammer Stirling Albion 6-1. What a great day. It was only one nothing at half time I think, and Craig, who was also there was so cold and fed up that he left to go to the pub and missed a great second half. What a day.

But back to our present adventures, we had decided to get the bus along Great Western Road and visit a pub called 'Oran Mhor'. Craig had never been in it before. It has won the pub of the year award this year, I think. The reason I suggested going there was because it is the type of pub that Craig hates. It is a converted church, beautiful inside and is frequented by the mainly well to do theatre types and other famous local Scottish celebrities. I had no trouble talking Craig into visiting it. I think Craig wanted to see someone famous.

The pub was very nice, but the price of the pints was about double what we were paying in the other pubs we had visited. This and the no celebrities turning up wasted it for Craig. It is a beautiful building and pub mind you.

Barman Rating; 🍺🍺 (and that's for letting us in)

Craig; We were now in an area called Partick. I thought we had already been there but I was just confused. All the whirling around on the underground was beginning to scramble my brain. The beer might also have been a factor.

When John told me we were going to Walter Smith's pub, The Rosevale I was a wee bit concerned. I was imagining a vision in red, blue and white, with maybe a flute band playing special requests for the shell suited patrons. The pub itself was neat and clean. Other than that it was pretty unspectacular. I do remember that the toilet was downstairs, not quite the bowels of the earth, but close enough. This is not an arrangement I would encourage in pubs. Like most people who enjoy the occasional beer of an evening, or afternoon for that matter, I tend to get a little less mobile as the session goes on. Strangely, stairs seem to become steeper at the same time.

After listening to me bleating on about my aversion to the basement facilities, John decided he couldn't face the stairs so he put on a pantomime limp and hobbled into the disabled toilet behind the bar.

'The Gazelle', according to John, was a great, down to earth, working man's pub. I was delighted. It would be full of characters from the shipyards with great stories to tell of the hey day of ship building on the Clyde. There would be photographs of historic liners and maybe some old fixtures and fittings from some of the famous warships fitted out there. It was rubbish!

According to the barmaid the pub had just reopened a couple of weeks ago after a complete makeover. In my opinion whoever did the making over was suffering from a serious hangover, or a complete lack of taste. If the choice of décor wasn't deranged enough the standard of finish was totally unbelievable.

The bar surface had been varnished, but it had never been sanded down. It felt like sandpaper to the touch. You could take the skin off your arm if you brushed against it. On the plus side however, your glass would be unlikely to slide off the bar. Even the new flat screen telly had been put up on the wall at a squinty angle. How the hell did no one notice that?

Obviously I had never clapped eyes on this pub before the renovations but if I was to guess I would say that there must have been at least 50 quid's worth of improvements made to the bar. And you can really stretch that out if you use the discount bins at B&Q.

John; We left and headed down Byres hoping to get a bus that would save us the 80p single on the Subway. Why we bother trying to save 80p when we are spending about a thousand pounds on drink escapes me.

With no buses in sight, we went into Hillhead Subway Station and grudgingly paid the money to get us to Partick and back to the kind of pubs we prefer, old men's pubs.

178

Coming out of the bus station at Partick and into Dumbarton Road, you are spoiled for choice if you are looking for a good pub, which we were. We decided to go into '*The Rosevale*'. It was nice, a bit too nice. I have a feeling that since they built all the new up market flats along the side of the Clyde, just behind Dumbarton Road, that the décor in some of the old pubs has changed, and not for the better. It is hard for me to explain what I am complaining about, it's just that the 'Rosevale' seems more up market than it used to be, trying to attract more couples. I may be wrong and there's nothing wrong if that's what they are doing.

In this type of pub, you're not encouraged to stand at the bar, I think the owners think it makes the place look messy, especially if it's Craig and I. So we had no conversation with the barman.

The pints were good mind you and the price, although more expensive than the first few pubs we were in, was not too bad. As another wee aside, I think that '*The Rosevale*' used to be owned, or part owned by Rangers ex manager, Walter Smith, (or Sir Walter or God, if you're talking to a Rangers fan.)

Barman Rating; ▉▉.

Back at the bus station we found a bus that would take us through the Tunnel to Govan, saving us the 80p Subway fare. The enjoyment we get from saving this money is out of all proportion to the amount saved. I think we're both a bit daft! The even better thing about the bus was that it went through Linthouse, where I was brought up and where I drank for a couple of years before moving to '*Mac's Bar*', in Govan. Although Mac's is long since closed, '*The Gazelle*' in Linthouse is still there. So I had a nostalgic walk along the old shops in Linthouse and into '*The Gazelle*'. What a let down. The pub had just been completely refurbished and smelled of paint and varnish. The floor was varnished wood and it was obvious they were trying to go up market. What's happening to our pubs? Why won't owners be happy just to give them a clean every now and again and put the bleach down in the morning to give the impression, or smell, of it just having been cleaned.

The only good thing was that I found out that an old pal of mine, Bill McLelland is still alive and to the fore. He is working in the local Hospital and comes in for a drink some mornings. I was delighted and surprised that Bill was still alive. The amount he used to drink was amazing. Good on you Bill. Would try to get in touch, but Bill definitely won't be on Facebook or those other new-fangled web things, or will he?

Apart from the modern décor, the beer was good and the barman was good company and helpful.

Barman Rating; ░░░░.

Craig; Govan was calling. This really was John's old stamping ground, or so he kept telling me. Funny thing was he didn't seem to know his way around it. I suppose you have to take urban redevelopment into account, as well as his advancing years of course.

We eventually found a pub he claimed to remember. 'Brechins' was a good, honest working man's pub. I don't suppose much has changed in that place in the last twenty years, fabulous!

Back in the city centre we stopped off for a quick brew in Ross's. It's a reasonable, slightly upmarket, sort of bar, perhaps a little bit bland but good all the same. What we really needed was something good to eat. That's not what we got.

For some reason John thinks 'The Blue Lagoon' fish and chip shop is a great place to eat. Although for some strange reason, after a certain number of beers, he insists on calling it 'The Blue Dolphin'. Personally speaking I've had the odd single fish from that shop which tasted as if they were using something other than haddock in batter, but then again I usually have a beer or two in me by that time as well.

We bought a couple of bags of creash with some chips floating around in them and made our way to the station.

Back in the Monty we had an night cap or two, simply for the sake of tradition you understand. We were then transported safely home by Irene.

Our day had started out as a bit of an anti-climax. Up until twelve hours before we started out we had thought Loch Lomond was to be our main destination of the day.

It was probably a good thing that I didn't have a long time to think about this Glasgow Outer Circle trip. This quickly arranged trip meant that we would be visiting some areas of Glasgow which I have been trying to avoid for many years. Actually I'm glad that things worked out the way they did. As it turned out the pubs we visited were very much like the ones we have found all over the place. Some were good, some were very good and of course some were manky. Welcome to Glasgow.

John; I was feeling very nostalgic as we left (I think the drink was kicking in) and got a bus the short trip into Govan. I didn't recognize any of it as the developers destroyed most of it before people realized that doing up buildings, like they have now done in other areas, is much better than pulling everything down and replacing them with crap buildings.

Having said all that, I managed to find one of Govans' oldest and best known pubs, *'Brechin's'*. Inside, it is just as I remembered, nothing has changed. The bar is in the centre of the pub and is round. I don't think a thing has changed in over 40 years, great.

It was brilliant to know that some things are forever. We enjoyed our pints in an atmosphere of nostalgia, remember we had a few inside us by then. The only down side was that there was nobody in the pub I knew. Mind you, it's been about 40 years. I asked the barman if he remembered a few names I mentioned, but I don't think he was even born then. He was very pleasant though.   **Barman Rating;** RR.

Leaving the pub, we wandered round to Govan Cross to find the Subway Station. It seemed to be in a different place to where it was before, but it's just that everything around it is different. It was a bit depressing and I was glad to get back on the Subway for our last journey of the day underground back to St. Enoch's Square. One great thing about the Subway is that if it is going to where you are going, if you know what I mean, it gets you there in no time at all.

Checking our watches, we worked out that we had time to drop in for a swift one before getting our train home. Don't know why we bothered as there's no time on our watches when we wouldn't have had time to nip in for a pint, or two. We stopped into *'Ross's'* on Mitchell Lane. I've been in it a few times and it's a nice pub. They do a great pint of Export, which was off. So we had the usual Lager and Best, went over the happenings of the day to try and remember where we had been and then left and bought chips in 'The Blue Lagoon', I think it's called.

It's a funny thing, the chips there are always soft, white and look terrible, but they taste great, especially after a few pints.

After eating the chips on the train, which must annoy the hell out of the other passengers, especially the drunk ones, we got off in EK and wandered up to *'The Monty'*.

We had a couple there then Craig's Irene picked us up and drove me right to the door. I think she worries that if she doesn't take me right to the door, I might sneak off and have another pint.

Kate's sister Sheila was staying with us that night so Kate had company and did not miss me too much, although if you knew me you'd know she must.

So another great trip was over, a trip which took in some of the real places in Glasgow, where real men and bigots still live in harmony. Come on the Thistle.

In Summary

When planning this trip we had to be very selective. There are hundreds of fine pubs in Glasgow. Unfortunately there are also a fair number of real honkers as well. As it was we accidentally managed to visit a cross section of these two categories.

It started off well enough but faded away a bit after that. Then again, maybe it was us doing the fading.

We thought that our little birl around the city might turn out to be a bit of a historical jaunt. That part was really quite successful as we found that the patrons in the first two pubs on our list have been singing the same old songs since the 17th century, if you know what we mean.

We also managed to find a pub which catered for the more refined drinker. So obviously we stuck out like a pair of sore thumbs in there. It has to be said that there is an awful distance between these two ends of the drinking spectrum and somewhere in the middle is where we like to 'hing aboot'. Notwithstanding our attempt to gate crash a funeral parlour, a personal triumph of planning for John, there were very few real hiccups on this expedition of ours.

Our trip managed to gain a score of 3.12, putting Glasgow in 7th place in our league table. Since there are so many more pubs out there in the city, just waiting for a visit, we hope to one day improve that average score and move Glasgow up a place or two.

The Pub That Time Forgot

(Inverness is a richt touristy toon
Wi' plenty o' good pubs to rummle aroon.)

A; Blackfriars: B; Hootenanny:
C; The Gellions: D; Lauders:
E; McCallum's: F; The Market Bar
G; The Phoenix;

East Kilbride-Glasgow-Inverness
Glasgow-East Kilbride
Three Buses, One train

John; This was another trip that was decided at the last minute. It was only the day before that Craig and I decided to do a trip. We had recently done Aberdeen with success, meaning cheap drink. So I booked us on the 8.30am Gold Bus to Inverness the next morning.

This meant an early start, so I copied a hero of mine in a book I read recently and had a shower and shave before I went to bed so I could lie as long as possible. It still meant the alarm was set for 6.30am. As usual you don't sleep when you have to get up early in case the alarm doesn't go off. So I was up well before 6.30am. This doesn't happen to the hero in my book.

I had made the pieces the night before, so it was just a case of getting dressed, a quick breakfast and down for Craig at 7.00am. Craig's better half Irene complained about our early start. I told her she was daft and should phone Kate who was still in her kip. It doesn't make any difference to me as you cannot do much wrong with plain bread and corn beef (except miss the mustard).

So Craig and I wandered down to the bus stop. It was a nice morning and I felt wide awake despite the early start. The number 18 bus turned up on time and as I tried to put my bus pass onto the thing you put it on, it slipped down the side and the driver had a hell of a job getting it back. He was very nice about it which was a shock. Drivers are usually a shower of moaners. Mind you, considering the Jakies they have to put up with, who can blame them.

Craig had a great laugh at my expense. It didn't bother me as I knew I would get revenge later. I always do.

So we got to Buchanan Street Bus Station at about quarter past eight and wandered over to the bus stop. Although we were quite late arriving there was not much of a queue and we had no problem getting a nice seat. The Gold Bus is really nice, more like a luxury coach than a bus.

The Pub That Time Forgot

Craig; There is an obvious draw back to travelling on the Gold Bus. Although it is a great service and very comfortable, it is a fairly limited service. That means if you are interested in sampling local culture you really need to be on the earliest bus. In our case, that meant leaving the house at 7.00am to catch the number 18 bus into Glasgow Buchanan Bus Station. That is just an unearthly hour to be doing anything.

We had decided to make Inverness our destination for the day. There were two or three good reasons for this. John is convinced that the Gold Bus service cannot last much longer. The service is good, comfortable and very handy. Any one of these plus points could be enough to have it shut down. The second reason for visiting was a really simple one. We both like Inverness. I'd been there three times before and had enjoyed each visit. John had been to Inverness quite recently. It was while he was planning a wee holiday there with Kate that he discovered the Gold Bus service.

I think it was just a bit too early in the morning for John to be out and about. Quite often when we start out on one of our journeys John can get a wee bit carried away with the excitement of the occasion. He has been known to offer his credit card to the bus driver instead of his concessionary card. This usually fails to amuse bus drivers. Then again very little ever amuses them. On this occasion John managed to surpass himself. As he slapped his card down onto the card reader it slid off then slipped down between the machine and the perspex guard. There then followed a good three or four minutes of scrabbling about trying to get it back out. After a wee while I suggested that, if they really wanted, I could nip back to the house to get a screwdriver. I reckoned that I could have the ticket out of there in less than fifteen minutes.

John didn't laugh but, surprisingly, the driver did. He must be new to the job!

The Pub That Time Forgot

We made it into Glasgow with plenty of time to spare, despite John's ham-fisted card juggling routine. There were only twenty or so passengers waiting in the queue for the Gold Bus so we had no trouble finding decent seats. I spent the next half hour or so failing to complete the Sudoku puzzle in my newspaper. John entertained himself by reading his cherished Daily Mail. You could tell he was reading it because his lips were moving. I have tried to persuade him to buy a real newspaper but, he does like his comics. Still it keeps him quiet and, since it doesn't use big complicated words or concepts, it doesn't give him a sore head.

John; My brother Robert has a bed and breakfast in Inverness and I was looking forward to meeting up with him at some point of the day.

The journey was great with lots of laughs, especially at Craig and his eating fetishes. As you may know on the Gold Bus you get Tea or Coffee with scones or pancakes and shortbread to follow, all free.

Craig ordered the scone, which had flour sifted on the top and bottom of it, so it had to go. What a mess he made. I offered to lick it off. He didn't laugh. This was followed by him spilling the sugar all over the place. Craig eating is like a sketch from Faulty Towers.

So after the food was spread all over the bus, we settled down to admire the lovely scenery that we were going through.

On the road to Perth you pass Gleneagles, so I told Craig that the Johnny Walker Golf tournament had recently been played there. He was not impressed and told me that since Johnny Walker had closed their Bottling Plant in Kilmarnock he was having nothing to do with them and their products. Since Craig hates whisky I don't think it makes much difference. I asked him if they had opened a new 'prant' in China. He didn't appreciate my politically incorrect joke.

187

The road we were on for nearly all the journey was the A9. I have read a couple of times that statistically it is the most dangerous road in Scotland. Let me tell you right now that statement is a load of crap. There's nothing wrong with the road. It's the lunatic drivers that are the problem. Some of the passing manoeuvres you see them doing are ridiculous.

Glasgow to Inverness is one of the longest journeys in Scotland, and driving like a madman will reduce the time by about 10 minutes at the most, so what's the point? All you're doing is scaring the shit out of other motorists and probably getting some other driver killed.

The problem is that in today's politically correct world you cannot blame anybody for anything that happens, especially if they are splattered all over the road. So the A9 gets the blame. You have realized by now that I don't live in the politically correct world, I live in the real one which is populated by the over 60s.

It's a lovely journey up to Inverness and the views that you can see from the bus are much better than you see if you are driving. You pass places with great names like Drumuchtar Pass and Dalwhinnie. Another great one you pass is Slochd. It has a summit of 1315ft, I think. It is a wild place and I think you would need to be slochd to try and climb it.

Just before you get to Aviemore, you pass Newtonmore and then Kingussie. These are two towns famous for their Shinty Teams. Every year the BBC shows the final of some cup and it is usually between these two teams. It always surprises me that they broadcast it as there only seems to be about a dozen or so supporters scattered round the pitch, a bit like Scottish football nowadays.

Shinty always amazed me. The amazing part being that nobody gets killed. It's a really wild sport played by farmers and other hard men with sticks and no rules, well none I can work out.

The bus then turned off the A9 for a wee bit and stopped at Aviemore which is famous for climbing, hill walking, skiing and other sore things.

Kate has relatives, Billy and Gwenda who have a lovely second home there. Billy ran the drug squad for many years, then retired and bought the house in Aviemore using the contents of a suitcase. I'm only kidding. Billy is one of the nicest guys I've met, and if we want to continue getting invites to stay in their lovely house, Gangi Lodge, I better say nice things about him.

So after leaving Aviemore, it was only a short trip into Inverness, the Capital of the Highlands.

Craig; The steward came round to ask us what we wanted for refreshments. I asked for tea and John asked for coffee. We both got tea. The service is good but it's not perfect!

Just for a change I decided to have a scone with my tea. Big mistake!

I have been dabbling in the art of baking for about a year now, so if anyone knows a good scone when he sees one, it's me. Granted my area of expertise is to be found in the baking of cupcakes and fruit loaves but I still see myself as a bit of an authority on all baked goods.

The sorry looking object I was given was covered in flour. I hate this practice. As far as I'm concerned the ingredients are supposed to go inside the baked item. The prospect of coughing up clouds of finely sieved self-raising flour for the rest of the day didn't appeal to me, so I did what any normal person would do in the circumstances. I dusted it. To be honest I might have been a little obsessive in my dusting. It probably could be better described as a polishing action. John thought this was both strange and hilarious. The seat back table now had a thin coating of white powder covering most of its surface.

I had just finished scouring the scone when my tea arrived. To cut a long story short I managed to spill my sugar all over the table. Every time the steward passed our seats he glared at the mess I had made of the table. For some strange reason I felt guilty about this and tried to clean the place up a bit. Half the mixture of the flour and sugar ended up on my lap before I gave up on the idea.

About this time the bus hit a series of potholes. Tea was splattered all over me and the table, turning the mixture there into a gooey mess. Within a couple of minutes it had hardened like cement. I tried to scrape it off with my finger nails but couldn't shift it.

After we had picked up some passengers at Aviemore the steward came round again offering teas and coffees. He seemed a bit reluctant to offer me any. Who could blame him? I decided not to push my luck and opted for a soft drink instead, only spilling a tiny drop of it down the front of my shirt.

John; Inverness is a lovely city, at least I think it's now a city. As usual the town planners and architects have tried their best in recent years to build large structures using concrete and no imagination. However it is still a lovely city and as Craig and I got off the bus the sun was out, which makes everything even nicer.

Craig, as usual, had been on the Google Earth thing and found out the names and locations of about a hundred pubs. What a man.

The first pub we tried was called '*Blackfriar's*'. This is a really great pub with a very friendly and helpful barman called Del. When we told him that we had written a book about our travels, he asked if he could see one. Luckily I had one with me which he promptly bought, gave us his business card and asked us to get him a copy of our next book (the one you are now reading) when it comes out.

We spoke to an English tourist who was travelling around the north of Scotland, staying, where possible, at bed and breakfasts or small hotels with pubs attached. He was a right chatterbox but a really nice bloke who enjoys his own, and everyone else's company.

We had a couple of pints and the time passed really quickly. We were sad to leave but knew we were not here to enjoy ourselves but to research places and pubs and report to our readers. So off we went to find our next pub.

Barman Rating;  (automatic if you buy a book)

Craig; By the time we got off the bus in Inverness it must have looked like I'd been rolling around a bakery floor. It was time for a beer. I had made an extensive list of likely pubs and their locations so it didn't take us long to find Blackfriar's Highland Bar.

John enjoys an endless supply of the brackish water he calls beer.

That name annoyed me more than a little as it screamed 'tourist'. That being said, Inverness is a major tourist destination so, it should come as no surprise that they tend to cater for them.

The bar was very traditional, with no obvious 'tourist tat' on display. It was also empty. I felt very comfortable in the place as soon as we walked in the door. Apparently there is entertainment on in the bar every night. There is an extensive range of real ale and malt whisky available. What a pity I can't stand either.

The barman, Del, was very friendly and asked us what we were up to in the town. I told him about the book and John, just to prove we weren't shooting a line, fished out a copy of the book from my rucksack. Del was so impressed he insisted on buying it there and then. It was the only copy we had with us but, a sale is a sale, so we sold it.

The whole idea of taking a copy of the book with us was to show it round the pubs in an attempt to drum up some trade. Now after only twenty minutes in the city we had flogged it. John was a wee bit huffed that he wasn't asked to autograph our masterpiece.

While we were drinking our very acceptable beers we got talking to an English chap who was one of those real ale addicts. They always remind me of train spotters. I like beer, I drink beer. What I don't do is witter on about it for hours on end. This fellow bases his entire two weeks summer holiday around finding the top twenty real ale pubs in Britain. He had a list and was ticking them off.

After another pint, to celebrate selling the book, we decided it was time to move on as we also had a list which needed some ticking.

John; *'The Hootananny'* is one of Invernesses most famous pubs and has won the award of 'Scotland's best Scottish Music Venue, 2005'. The reason I know this piece of highland information is that it is engraved above the pub in huge letters. I wonder who has won it since then. There was no music on when we went in, but it was only about one o'clock so a bit early for the teuchter music. The pub was very quiet and had no atmosphere. There was no one behind the bar who seemed to know what they were doing and nobody acknowledged we were in the place.

We managed a pint and left. It is a nice enough looking place and I'm sure it will be jumping at night when the music starts, definitely not a daytime man's pub and the barman, a young foreign gentleman I think showed no interest in talking to us.

Barman rating; .

We wandered down to the river, found a bench and had our pieces in the sunshine. There were one or two seagulls about so I made sure I didn't throw my crusts into the water as if you do you know that you would be engulfed in gulls. The guy on the next bench must have been annoying Craig, although god knows why as he was sitting quietly minding his own business. As we got up and passed his bench Craig told me to drop a few crusts behind this bloke's seat. When we looked back only one seagull had flown down so Craig didn't get the satisfaction of the man being attacked by a flock of gulls.

The river area is very nice and the seagulls don't bother you too much. I then remembered to phone my brother and arranged to meet up with him in our next pub which was *'The Cellion's'*.

This pub was on the main road leading to the bridge and I think it relied on tourists for its trade as there was not a lot of atmosphere and I couldn't imagine a lot of locals using it as their regular haunt. There was nothing wrong with the pub that you could put your finger and we enjoyed our pint. Robert and Ruth (his better half) arrived just as we were about to leave so we asked him to take us to a decent local pub. By that we meant and old man's pub.   **Barman Rating;** .

Craig; John had been telling me about a pub he had been in, or seen, the last time he had visited Inverness. It was called

193

'Hootenanny'. I was instantly less than thrilled. The pub claimed to be the best traditional music venue in Scotland. I still wasn't impressed. Anyway, we decided to give it a go. It looked more like a café than a real bar.

It was slightly disconcerting to find a Taiwanese barman in charge of one of Scotland's premier traditional music venues. In fact very little about this place looked traditional. I had expected a lot of kilts, bagpipes and shortbread. We didn't stay long.

A hoot it was not.

John's favourite tipple is a pint of Best which, in my opinion, is only slightly more alcoholic than rainwater. Unfortunately he couldn't get his favourite drink in the first two pubs and he had to settle for some strange, but strong, substitute. It was one of those real ale concoctions, brewed from nettles and insoles

The Pub That Time Forgot

from old hiking boots. These evil brews taste like crap but are very potent. After only three pints he was feeling the difference. I thought I might have to tie a string to his ankle to stop him floating away.

To make sure he didn't lose the plot too early on in the day we decided it would be a good idea to take a break for some food. Down at the River Ness we found an unoccupied bench and had our sandwiches. Making conversation, I might have said something to the effect that if you really wanted a bit of a laugh it would be funny to drop pieces of bread behind a bench someone was sitting on. The seagulls which were circling over our heads would then swoop down for a feed, frightening the life out of the poor guy on the bench. It was meant to be hypothetical of course but I'm afraid that John has a very shaky understanding of the meaning of the word hypothetical.

I can only think it was the change of beer but, the next thing I knew, John was throwing bread crusts behind the bench of an innocent bystander. Fortunately for everyone concerned, the seagulls of Inverness seem to be remarkably well fed and failed to attack.

This part of the town is very picturesque with great views of the river, its bridges and some very nice older buildings on the far bank. It's a pity about the southern side of the river.

Inverness Castle sits on a hill overlooking what I would imagine is the town centre. The castle is not very imposing. Maybe they didn't get much trouble up this way in medieval times.

The town centre is a monument to what can be achieved when planners have access to limitless amounts of cash and concrete. There may well be some really fine buildings in there somewhere, but they would be overpowered by the big 'Lego' like office buildings. It must have taken a team of architects an entire lunch break to come up with the design.

The Pub That Time Forgot

We crossed the bridge to visit a pub I remembered from a previous visit to the town. The Glenalbyn was, as far as I could recall, a great wee pub, very welcoming and bright. We walked in one door and straight out of the other. Maybe my memory is starting to go, it was nothing like the pub I remembered.

Back across the bridge we visited The Gellions. It was a bit more modern than we had assumed. The young barmaid was very chatty, unfortunately she confined her chattiness to her pal at the far end of the bar. I felt as if we were intruding when I asked for a couple of beers. She served them quickly, barely missing a beat in her conversation with her friend.

John's brother and his wife came in just as we were finishing our drinks. I suggested that maybe we should find another pub, perhaps one where they didn't resent serving customers.

It's amazing how the architects managed to blend the old with the new. Wearing a blindfold probably helped.

The Pub That Time Forgot

John; Robert and Ruth took us to *'Lauder's'*. The four of us had a good chat and I managed to catch up with what was happening to the brother and his B & B business. Everything is going great and business is on the up. I was really pleased as I was a bit worried with the recession and everything. The pub itself was ok although nothing really special. It would be unfair to rate the barman as the four of us were chatting all the time.

We said a farewell to Ruth who was going to have her hair done and the three of us wandered up the road and into *'MacCallum's'*. This is a great pub with fantastic pieces of memorabilia decorating the place from floor to ceiling. In the middle of all this atmospheric stuff there was a working electric fireplace which looked only about a year or so old. We had no idea why it was there. There was no heat coming from it. It was so out of place and crappy looking that it was fantastic. The people who arranged the decorating of this pace must be really weird.

We were starting to have a really great time, partly because by this time we had about six pints inside us. I think we only had one pint, but it was a really great pub and would advise anybody visiting Inverness to look it up, even just to see the fireplace. The guy behind the bar was very friendly and the service was good. **Barman rating;** 🍺🍺🍺🍺.

Craig; That's how we ended up in 'Lauders' It was quite a reasonable pub and the beer was very acceptable. I was a wee bit confused when we stepped through the door of the place I have to say. It was a very strange set up where you almost have to sway to get in through the doorway. Usually I do a fair bit of that on the way out of a pub. It took me a couple of minutes to realise that it was actually a revolving door which had been wedged open. Drunks usually have enough trouble getting through a conventional door, revolving doors must cause chaos at shutting time. It would be worth visiting Lauder's just to watch the worthies trying to negotiate the birling door after a right good session.

We asked Robert to show us a couple of the more colourful boozers in the area. I'm happy to say he was up to the task. MacCallum's was the first one on his list. From the outside this pub looked more like a 1960s barber shop. I have no idea why anyone other than a not too fashionable barber would decorate their front window with black and white photographs of dodgy looking old pop stars. It was a bit quirky on the inside as well. They certainly go in for what might be described as unique décor, but it works very well.

Are these pictures of people who are barred, and will there be another three photos going up soon?

John; As far as old men's pub's go, Robert had saved the best for last. We went into *'The Market Bar'*. What a place. There were about half a dozen guys of about our age around the bar.

As soon as we wandered in and ordered our pints everybody wanted to know who we were and why we were there. It was great and I got some fantastic handshakes. We had a great time talking to all the locals and if I lived in Inverness, I think this would be my local. Although I should be clear and say that the three pubs we were in previously were great and would probably suit most sensible people.

When you are in the company of drunks and are enjoying yourself you know, or should know, it is getting to the time when you should get out before the enjoyment goes too far. This was starting to happen, so Robert, the soberest, suggested to Craig and I that it was time to go. I should add that Robert is 10 years younger than me, and might have been worried about any reputation he has. **Barman rating;** 🍺🍺🍺🍺🍺.

**One of our new friends from the Market Bar.
A couple of beers solved the language barrier.**

So with great sorrow and twenty minute handshakes all round we staggered out into the Inverness streets and I think (I am not at all sure) that we went into one more pub, *'The Pheonix'*. I have no recollection of what it was like, but Craig assures me that we had a pint and it was quite a nice wee pub. I've no idea. Craig said the barman was ok and worth three Russells.

Barman rating; 🍺🍺🍺.

Craig; I can't actually remember how we got into the Market Bar, but I'm glad we did. Since we got back from this trip I have been trying to find the pub on my computer. It's not there. I've got the correct address, 32 Church Street, but when I check it on Google street level, it doesn't exist. Maybe it's like Brigadoon and only appears when you've swallowed enough beer. It's certainly a magic wee place.

I don't think I've ever been in a friendlier pub. We swapped stories with the locals, most of them unrepeatable, and laughed ourselves silly. Someone mentioned that the bar opened at nine in the morning. If true that would explain an awful lot.

It would have been very easy to stay there in the Market, but we had to move on. So we left the bar, to a round of applause, and re-entered the real world through the secret door.

Robert had one last pub to show us. The Phoenix was to be our last pub of the day, in Inverness at least. Even through the slight haze caused by a really good bevy session, I realised that the Phoenix was directly across the road from our first pub of the day, Blackfriars.

Inverness must either be a really small city or we were very fortunate that all the very best pubs are within staggering distance of each other.

The Phoenix was a good pub to end our little trip. It was clean, well decorated and sold a good pint. Beyond that I couldn't really comment as my memory was slightly impaired due to excessive enjoyment.

John; It was with great sadness, Craig told me the next day, that we said goodbye to Robert and wandered back to the bus station. I think the driver and the Hostess (the girl who gives you your scone and tea) knew we had a wee bevy in us as she kept an eye on us to make sure we didn't have a carry out on us. We didn't. It was great having the toilet on the bus, although I only went once during the three and a half hour journey. The bladder is still to the fore.

The journey back down the A9 passed without incident, although we both dozed off and on all the way back to Glasgow. By the time we arrived back in Buchanan Street bus station it was getting dark. This was the 31st of August, the last day of summer.

It was about four hours since our last pint and I was getting the feeling of a hangover starting, so the only thing to do was to pop into *'The Horsehoe'* for a pint or two to get rid of the hangover.

Kate texted me while we were enjoying our pints and offered to pick us up at EK train station. So at 10.20pm we arrived back in EK. Craig fancied dropping into *'The Lum'* on our way home, but I knew Kate thought I was pretty drunk and I thought better of it. Just shows you I was not that drunk.

So ended our trip to Inverness and I must say it is a great place with some great pubs, *'Blackfriar's', 'MacCallum's'* and *'The Market Bar'* being the pick of the bunch.

Craig; Back on the bus we settled down to our long journey home. I was very careful to avoid all contact with floury scones and potentially scalding tea. Falling asleep almost immediately helped me accomplish this.

When we arrived back in Glasgow I was keen to make my way straight to Central Station, but time was against us. We were walking along Renfield Street, quite close to the Horse Shoe Bar, when John informed me that we couldn't make it to the station in time for the next train. Quick as a flash, we decided to cut our losses and go for a beer. Unfortunately, while we were still inside the Horse Shoe, we miss timed things yet again and missed another train.

Kate very kindly came down to East Kilbride station to pick us up, bringing to an end yet another great day out and about in some of Scotland's best pubs. Inverness turned out to be a really good destination for us two beer tippling travellers.

We have in the past tended to avoid the North East of Scotland. It has always had a reputation, among west coasters at least, for being a bit dour and unfriendly.

However less than a month ago we spent a great day in Aberdeen which went some way to dispel that notion. Inverness surpassed even that trip for friendliness and great beer. And, after all, those are the two main ingredients in a really special day out.

In Summary

The capital of the highlands has a lot going for it. From the famous Loch Ness to Culloden there's plenty to see. But it was probably the chance to travel on our old favourite, the Gold Bus, which decided us on making this trip.

The majority of the pubs we visited were pretty good. Of course there was also a couple of them you couldn't force us back into at gunpoint. But that is par for the course in any of the places we visit.

The biggest problem with travelling long distances on a day trip is that you have to leave for home just when things are getting interesting. On the plus side, there's always that great bus to look forward to.

Although, if you've spent your time wisely, appreciating all the culture, magnificent architecture and of course the good cheer provided by a few friendly publicans you'll probably manage a couple of hours sleep on the journey home. We certainly did.

Dundee-a piece o' cake

(Dundee's just great, I am a fan
We ate and drank like Desperate Dan.)

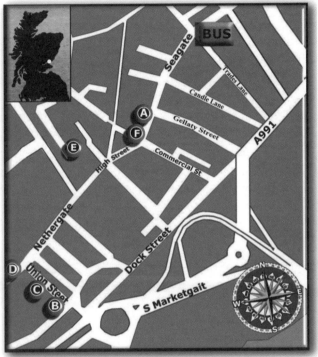

A:- Bush Bar,   B:- Club Bar:
C:- The Bank Bar, D:- The Phoenix,
E:- The Artic Bar, F:- Tickety Boo's:

*East Kilbride-Glasgow-Dundee-Glasgow-East Kilbride
(Three Buses, One Train, One Taxi)*

Dundee-a Piece o' Cake

John; Having visited Aberdeen and Inverness, the last big town, or city that we had not been to was Dundee. So it was Dundee that we planned to explore on this latest trip.

It was a fairly easy trip to plan, I went on the web and looked up the bus times and Craig went on Google and checked up on the position of the pubs.

We decided to leave a bit later than usual as Craig was having a late night and I had to run Kate and her sister Sheila (the bevy merchant) into Glasgow to catch the 9 o'clock Gold Bus to Aberdeen. They were going to visit their friend Sandra and stay overnight with her.

This meant that I had an empty house and could come home late and in any state without Kate knowing. To cut a long story short, Kate phoned me the next morning and could tell by my voice exactly how many pints I had. I couldn't argue as I had no idea how many I had, but it was a lot.

After getting up at about 7 o'clock and running the two sisters into Glasgow, I got myself ready (Kate had made my pieces) and wandered down to Craig's in brilliant sunshine. The past two days had been terrible as we had caught the tail of some hurricane or other. Forgot what it was called.

The usual number 18 bus ran us into Glasgow. The only thing of note on the bus, and for the rest of the day, was Craig continually whipping out his new phone. It is one of those that can do anything, mind you, about 99% of the things it does are a complete waste of time. But this didn't stop Craig. He is a gadget nut.

As well as Craig having a late night, Sheila and I downed about a bottle and a half of red wine, so Craig and I both had a touch of the munchies. So it was into the shop in the bus station to buy crisps for Craig and Bombay mix for me. It's amazing the rubbish you feel like when you have the munchies.

The sun was out and it was a lovely day as the bus left Glasgow and headed north, passing places like Stirling, Perth and eventually into Dundee. It was a great journey and the scenery was brilliant. A bit of advice here, Bombay Mix is a nightmare to eat on a bus and by the time we had reached Perth the floor at our feet was like a beach, Bombay mix everywhere. On the way into Dundee we passed a huge and very famous sailing ship called The Discovery, although I've no idea why it's famous and I didn't want to ask Craig as he would have whipped out the new phone. I got a great picture of it from the speeding bus which really annoyed Craig who takes ages over each picture. You probably won't get a chance to see the picture as Craig is in charge of which ones we print. For Craig to get as good a picture he would have been setting up the camera as we passed Perth.

Dundee is famous for a lot of things. Linoleum, Marmalade, Jute, I think, 'The Broons, Oor Wullie and The Sunday Post' spring to mind, after half an hour trying to remember. Nothing springs quickly to my mind nowadays.

Craig; *I'm happy to say that our latest journey to the east of Scotland didn't have to start off at an ungodly hour of the morning. Heading out east usually means an early start for us and, this has been pointed out to me on many occasions, I'm not a morning person. Dundee is only about an hour and a half away from Glasgow by bus. This meant a good long lie in for me, and it was much appreciated. The night before our trip I had enjoyed my usual Tuesday night up at Auldhouse listening to some great music. Just to be sociable I had tipped back a few beers and therefore required an extra bit of time to sleep off any possible after effects.*

We have travelled down to Glasgow on the number 18 bus so often recently that I don't even bother looking out of the windows anymore. Actually, if you've ever driven through Rutherglen you'll appreciate what a good idea that is.

John had once again created a schedule for us to follow. Personally, I thought that a spread sheet detailing the arrival and departure of a single bus was a bit of overkill, but John really loves his spread sheets.

The Citylink bus to Dundee was a bit of a disappointment. It's not that it was uncomfortable or anything like that. The reason for my disappointment was in the comparison between the standard Citylink coach and the fabulous Gold Bus we have been travelling on recently. We do like a wee bit of luxury.

Of course our journey on this economy class bus was made a bit worse by some of our travelling companions. It's hard to believe that an entire family of five can all be stone deaf so I have to conclude that they just enjoy making such an ear splittingly loud racket when they talk to each other. To make sure we got the full stereo sound effect of their constant roaring, they spread themselves across a number of seats on either side of the bus. The male elder of the tribe decided to add to the mayhem by sharing his music with the rest of us passengers.

I'm not sure which particular device he was using to broadcast his music but it sounded like the speakers must have been made out of tissue paper, stretched over a biscuit tin. His taste in music also left a lot to be desired. It was definitely more X-Factor than classic rock. Actually when their baby started wailing it was like a breath of fresh air.

John managed to miss almost all of this nonsense as he had lapsed into unconsciousness soon after leaving Glasgow. As far as he is concerned Dundee is only thirty minutes away from Glasgow.

John; So we got off the bus at the bus station and wandered off in the direction that Craig said all the pubs were. He had found them on his new phone.

This new phone of his is really great cause the first pub we went into, called *'The Bush Bar'* turned out to be really brilliant, one of the best we have visited on our travels. What

206

makes a bar brilliant are the barman, the locals and the beer, and all were brilliant and a great laugh.

The barman, who was the owner, was a young guy called Harry who made us feel really welcome. As an added bonus he bought one of the two books we had brought with us. Another of the locals called Donald gave us the money for another. We took a note of his address and are going to send him one. These Dundee people are a trustworthy lot. We didn't want to give him our last one, although for the life of me I can't think why. It was Craig's idea to keep one to show other people. Can't think why as we're not going to see them again.

Anyway, instead of our normal one, or possibly two pints and moving on, we had at least three pints and a great laugh with the locals. We got into the pub about half past one and we were still there at three when the daily Karaoke started. What a way to spend a day. The guy who gave us the money for the book on trust was desperate for us to stay so we could hear him sing one of Frank Sinatra's classics, I think. He said it was called 'The Shark Bite'. He went on and on about it and how good he was. I found this quite strange as he was sober. So up he went eventually and it turned out he was quite good. I think the only reason he gave us the money for the book was so we would stay to hear him.

Harry, the owner, had to leave and we promised to keep in touch. You do that when you're starting to get pissed. His replacement, a nice blond girl (I've forgotten her name) spent most of her time singing on the Karaoke machine. She only came down (it was up a couple of stairs) when someone, usually us, wanted a drink. She was great.

Talking about drink, a local bloke came in and Harry asked him if he was having a vodka, or a brandy. He ordered a brandy which Harry poured and put in front of him. He then went over to the gantry and picked up a bottle of port which he put down in front of the brandy. The guy picked up the bottle of port and poured a huge amount into his glass of brandy. What a man. I asked him later about his drink and he said it was quite a common drink in Dundee. I wonder if that's what 'Desperate Dan' drinks.

We would have been happy to have spent the day there, but we are consummate professionals and are visiting pubs, and towns, not to enjoy ourselves but to survey and take notes about the pubs and people we meet.

So it was with heavy hearts, and lighter wallets, that we said goodbye. There were tears all round and the blond girl sang 'We'll Meet Again'. At least that's how I remember it.

Barman Rating; 🍺🍺🍺🍺🍺, (he is worth even more but don't want to upset Russell).

Letting us behind the bar is a bit like giving a couple of weans the keys to the sweetie shop.

Craig; *By the time we got off the bus we were both ready for a beer. Fortunately, using my computer, I had memorised the locations of all the more interesting pubs in Dundee city centre. You just can't develop a skill like that, it's a talent. We walked along 'the Seagate' looking for our first pub of the day. That honour fell to the 'Bush Bar'.*

I would have to say that, just from looking at the outside of the building I wasn't overly impressed with the Bush. But as John has often said, "What the hell do you know?" I admit it, the Bush Bar is a brilliant wee pub.

The sign outside claimed that this was Dundee's Scottish pub, and it does not lie. It is exactly what I look for in a Scottish pub. There's plenty of reasonably priced booze on tap and the patter was great.

To be honest, when we first went into the pub, I got the distinct impression that we were in for a bit of a disappointment. The barman was a bit on the young side, compared to us anyway. We find that the bar staff tends to set the tone of the place. Young guys can be less than tolerant of us old yins and, I would have to admit, our humour doesn't always travel well.

It turned out that the young barman was very talkative, in a laid back sort of a way. We got talking about travelling as we almost always do and it turned out that Harry, our barman, had travelled around a large part of the world. That rather put our pathetic wee bus trips to shame. After listening to all his adventures in far flung places we were a wee bit embarrassed to show him our book. Actually, when I say we were embarrassed I really mean me. John is a man who knows no shame. I really didn't fancy our chances of flogging a book about two old geezers travelling around on the buses to someone who thinks nothing of driving an old motorbike across the Australian outback. Just shows you what I know. He liked the book and was quite happy to stump up the eight quid we

*were charging for it. This got the other customers interested
and they all wanted to have a look at it.*

*Our second customer of the day fancied himself as a bit of a
singer and insisted we stay to hear him when the karaoke got
going. I don't know what we would have done if he had turned
out to be absolutely pish at it. Fortunately he was quite good. I
hasten to add that my opinion was not influenced by him
buying one of our books. Of course we did make sure he paid
for it before he got up to sing, just in case.*

*Somehow we managed to knock back three pints in the Bush
Bar before we realised it was time to move on. We often take a
picture of the friendlier bar staff we meet so before we left I
suggested we should take a wee photo of Harry standing
behind the bar. He agreed but insisted that we should be in it
as well. When two of the customers volunteered to take the
pictures with our cameras I didn't bat an eye lid. In some of the
pubs we have visited recently that would have been the last we
would ever see of our cameras, but not here.*

*The three of us stood behind the bar, posing like 'haddies'
while our two cameramen snapped away. While it wasn't
exactly the paparazzi it was probably the closest we'll ever get
to being famous. God knows what any stranger walking in
would have thought of all the carry on.*

*It's not often that we find ourselves shaking hands with all the
customers in a bar we'd only just discovered, we usually try to
slink out without being noticed, but the Bush Bar is a special
case.*

John; We were both hungry by now and wandered up the main
street to find a nice seat in the sun to eat our pieces. On the way
we stopped at a statue of 'Desperate Dan', who is a character
made famous from the comic 'The Beano', I think. Craig asked
me to take a photo of him beside him. He is a real ugly big
man. Have a look at the photo and decide for yourself who I'm
talking about.

The sun was still shining and we found a bench in the centre of Dundee and enjoyed our pieces, Corned Beef and English Mustard on Plain Bread as usual. Craig had pieces, but he also had chicken bits on wooden sticks. He gave me one, it was delicious. I'll have to have a word with Kate about wee extras with my pieces.

I have never been into Dundee town centre before and I must say it is a really nice place and the area around seems to have a lot happening and there is a lot of new construction going on. It is definitely worth a visit.

**Getting a bit desperate for something to eat.
Cow pie or Chicken Satay?**

Harry had told us that the *'Club Bar'* was good, and the barmaid, Rachael was a friend of his and very good, we assumed he meant as a barmaid. So we took his advice and wandered down the road and into the 'Club'. The place was packed with locals when we went in. It was a nice pub and we introduced ourselves to Rachael as one of Harry's best pals. We still had to pay for the drink. After the 'Bush', it was always going to be difficult for any bar to measure up, but it was nice and we had a chat with Rachael, but the locals kept themselves to themselves. It was a good bar though, and worth the visit.

Barmaid Rating; 🍺🍺🍺.

Our next port of call was *'The Bank Bar'*. It was not bad inside, but the barman was very young and spent the time talking to his pal. This is a definite a no no and Craig took an instant dislike to the place, and the barman. Although the place was nice inside, and the beer was fine, we left as soon as we finished without as much as a 'how's it going' to anybody. That's how it goes sometimes.

Barman Rating; 🍺, (he's too young to care what we say)

Craig; We stopped in what I take to be the main square area of the city centre to have our sandwiches before moving on to our next pub. The Club Bar was a fairly nice pub with a friendly barmaid, Rachael, who chatted away quite happily to us. Unfortunately the customers weren't as boisterous as those up in the Bush bar but that didn't exactly surprise us too much. Once again we were pleased to find that the beer was reasonably priced but decided to make do with only one pint. We had after all a few more pubs to visit and, more importantly, the drinkers in this pub didn't look like the book buying types.

The Bank Bar was the next pub on our list to be visited and we were really happy that it was only a few minutes' walk back up the road. It was barely worth the effort. The bar was tidy enough but it had no real character. We were far from pleased with the staff as the young barman seemed very reluctant to get up off his arse to actually serve anyone. He seemed more content to chat to his pal at the far end of bar. We were given our drinks as quickly and quietly as our teenage barman could manage and, before we had a chance to annoy him any further, he scampered back along the bar to continue talking nonsense to his wee pal. That's what you get when businesses cut costs by employing child labour. As pubs go this one would make a good library. It was so quiet in the bar that we felt obliged to speak in whispers. I find this is always a good idea anyway, especially if you're slagging the place off as much as we were. It might have been interesting to find out about the history of this little bar but we couldn't find a responsible adult to ask so we finished our drinks and left.

John; *'The Phoenix'* was our next port of call and an ideal port of call for sailors. The place was very nice in a loud sort of way. Everything was a bit camp. I hope that's the politically correct way of saying it may have been a bar for members of the gay community. Having said that, it was nice and the two bar boys were nice and pleasant, and seemed to get on very well with each other, nice to see. There were some ladies in as well, so it may not only have been for the gay guys. But the new me enjoyed the banter and the happiness of the place. Not so sure about Craig as he's not as modern a man as I am.

While we were chatting to the bar boys we found out that the oldest pub in Dundee was just down the street and up an alley. So when we finished our pints, we bade everyone bon voyage and headed down the main street, up the appointed alley in search of our next destination. **Barman Rating:** ▦▦▦▦

We found *'The Arctic'* without any problems. It didn't look particularly old, outside or in. But after a chat with the barman, we were assured that this was a pretty old pub, but he had no proof that it was the oldest. I think the two boys in the last pub just wanted rid of us. We enjoyed our pints and it was a nice wee pub. Worth a visit if you can find the right alley.

Barman Rating; ▦▦▦▦, (he might have been the oldest barman in Dundee)

213

Things were starting to get a bit hazy. I think my last pint, about my tenth, might have been spiked, or I was getting drunk. I told Craig it was time to call it a day and head for the bus station. Amazingly, Craig agreed. So it was goodbye to the maybe oldest pub in Dundee and back to the bus station. However, after whipping out his phone, Craig told me we still had about 20 minutes till the departure, so instead of having a seat in the sun and waiting for the bus, like normal people would do, we decided to have one last pint in a pub called *'Tickety Boos'*. Honest, that was its name. As usual, after the amount I had drunk, I had no recollection the next morning of being in the place. If it wasn't for the photo of it in my camera, I would have had no idea we were in it at all. This happened to me once before, but that time it was a town, Kilmarnock that I could not remember visiting. Have to cut back on the bevy.

We must have finished our drinks, because we always do, and somehow managed to find our way back to the bus station and on to our bus.

Barman Rating; (what barman) **Craig's rating:** 🍺🍺🍺🍺

Craig; After a short walk we managed to find 'The Phoenix'. It was a very clean, tidy and modern pub, so we didn't particularly like it straight away. However, after a few minutes, we decided that it was really quite a nice wee place. The bar staff were really friendly, in fact they seemed to be having a much better time than anyone else in the pub. That's not always a good sign in a pub, but their patter was really good. They seemed quite interested in our project, or at least they managed to feign an interest. This is a talent which should be encouraged in trainees at bar staff training college.

We spoke to them about recommending a grottier pub for us to visit as so far all of Dundee's drinking establishments had been very tidy and orderly. A contrast was required. The guys behind the bar gave this some thought and eventually came up with 'The Arctic Bar'. This was the cue for everyone to start

214

trotting out inept jokes about maybe getting a cold reception, the cold shoulder or chilling out in that bar. I blame the drink. The Artic Bar is supposedly the oldest pub in Dundee.

That may or may not be true but I can assure you that it is one of the hardest to find.

It is hidden up a close and when you eventually find it you will understand why. Ugly is such a harsh word but, sometimes it is the only appropriate word. As you might imagine we had been wondering why anyone would call their pub 'the Arctic'. It just didn't make any sense to us, until we actually clapped eyes on it. It looked like a very large fridge freezer. Thankfully it was a different story inside.

A really cool joint? or just a cold reception.

One of the first things I noticed when we got into the bar was that, like every other pub in Dundee, karaoke seems to be very popular. I blame all this X-factor nonsense we are force fed on the telly and in the newspapers. What's wrong with dominoes? We enjoyed our drinks and chatted to the barman who

215

managed to avoid telling us anything at all about the history of his pub.

John had been a bit worried about this trip. His main concern had been the fact that we would be making our way home by bus. Usually we manage to organise things in such a way that the train takes the strain. The strain in question being bladder related. John doesn't like to get too far away from a working convenience when he's on an away day. Although he was fairly sure that our Citylink coach would have a W.C. he wasn't too keen on sharing it with another fifty odd passengers.

His master plan to avoid any chance of an excess fluid incident was to substitute his favourite tipple, a pint of Best, with a rather girly vodka and soda. This tactic might have worked a bit better if he hadn't started the day on draught beer. Switching to vodka half way through the shift meant he was breaking one of the cardinal rules of sensible boozing. He was mixing his drinks, and it was beginning to show.

John was getting a bit anxious about getting back to the bus station in plenty of time for our journey home. I suggested that he was just experiencing a vodka induced panic attack and steered him towards our next pub.

Normally I would never be seen anywhere near a pub called 'Tickety Boo's'. It just sounds like such a vodka and tonic sort of a place. Not my scene at all. I'm really glad we went in though. It was a bit wine barish but we really enjoyed our short stay there, even if not all of us remembered it.

The barman was friendly efficient and professional, proved by the fact that he didn't so much as snigger when I ordered a half pint. This led us on to an animated discussion about alcoholic units in different drinks. It got so ridiculous that the barman got a calculator out to prove his point, whatever that was. We had passed the point of understanding mathematical equations several stops before this one. Once again we had found a great wee pub with a barman who was up for a laugh.

The barman calculates that John has had enough.

John; As soon as the bus left the station I was sound asleep. I was woken with a start when the bus stopped. We were in Perth town centre. The bus on the way to Dundee didn't stop anywhere so this was obviously a different bus. Craig had his magic phone out to check if we were on a bus that would end up in Glasgow and he assured me that this was the right bus.

The next thing I knew was that the bus had stopped again. This time it was in Stirling Bus Station. I had slept all the way. This was annoying Craig as he thought I should be enjoying the trip. I managed to stay awake for the rest of the trip which included a detour through Cumbernauld. The bus didn't stop there which was just as well, Cumbernauld is a real ugly place, although the people are nice.

When we arrived back in Glasgow, we were both feeling recovered and ready to face more bevy. As normal, we wandered down West Nile Street and into *'The Horseshoe'* and enjoyed a couple of pints as we decided which train we would get home so we would still have time to visit 'The Monty' in East Kilbride.

While we were in *'The Horseshoe'*, there was a Champions league match on between Manchester City and some Italian team, I think. We were not watching the game, but heard a big cheer when the Italian team scored. Shortly afterwards another big cheer went up, and when we looked, Manchester City had scored. What's that all about? We're in the centre of Glasgow and people are going nuts over foreign teams. Funny thing is that I'm pretty sure all the people in the pub were from Glasgow.

Eventually nobody will go to football matches and will decide who they support by how nice their strips are, or something like that. All the hatred and bigotry will disappear. Is that a good thing?

We eventually left the pub and wandered over to the Central Station and caught the 10.18pm train to East Kilbride. We had worked out that if we could get to 'The Monty' by 10.50pm we would still be able to get a pint as we reckoned the pub shut at 11.00pm. I can't remember when the pub shut but I think we had a couple, so it must have been well after eleven when we left. I remember the barman shouting at us to get out. What a cheek.

As walking was a problem and it was late, we jumped a taxi home. Not only was Kate away in Aberdeen but Craig's Irene was out babysitting so nobody knew if we were drunk or not.

So it was off to bed on my own after a great day spent in the historic city of Dundee.

Dundee-a Piece o' Cake

Craig; *We arrived back at the bus station with a good ten minutes to spare. Just in case John had a point about sharing facilities on the bus, I decided to visit the toilet, and was promptly charged twenty pence for the experience. This, to my mind at least, is sheer profiteering. It's not as if it was luxurious in there. Although, given that there were three people in the kiosk I bought my ticket from, I can see where the money goes.*

The journey home was a wee bit annoying as the driver seemed determined to visit every bus stop between Dundee and Glasgow. While I was suffering this, John had decided to spend the time in deep meditation. I can only assume he was meditating on the benefits and or drawbacks of mixing your drinks.

Needless to say he was feeling much refreshed by the time we arrived back in Glasgow. So obviously he needed a wee refreshment in the Horse Shoe Bar. Over a couple of drinks we reviewed the events of the day, and I filled him in on the bits he had missed.

Since there was no hurry to get home we stopped off for a quick one in the Monty in East Kilbride. I almost feel sorry for the poor taxi driver who pulled the short straw and had to take us up the road from the pub. Both John and I were by this time working without a volume control. I was trying to be clever and John was speaking Latin.

Our latest journey had turned out to be yet another great day out. Dundee has suffered from a bad reputation in the past but, as far as we are concerned, it has turned that around and is now a great place to visit. The pubs were all clean and tidy and the city itself looked great. We assume that a great deal of money has been spent recently on its redevelopment.

Almost everywhere we visited the people went out of their way to be helpful and friendly. The thing which impressed us most would have to be the quality of the city's bar staff, very professional. The one blot on this rosy picture of Dundee's licenced trade was the bar where we were grudgingly served by that wee boy who obviously didn't see the bar trade as a future career choice. Fortunately, for the city's boozeaholics, as soon as the summer holidays are finished the plooky faced, work shy wee bugger will probably be back at school.

In Summary

We had quite a good day out in Dundee, for the most part. The city is in the process of some serious redevelopment and is beginning to shape up to be a really worthwhile place to visit. Apparently there are a lot of things to see and do in and around the place. However we were far too busy to find any of them. We were on a mission.

On our day out we found that most of the pubs there were well above average. With one glaring exception we enjoyed the hospitality on offer. Actually it takes a lot to put us off our stride on one of our beer sampling adventures, but inattentive barmen are high on the list of things that really annoy us.

Using our wildly inaccurate Russell Standard of bar ratings Dundee would have come out joint top of all the booze emporiums we have visited if it hadn't been for that wee lazy boy in The Bank Bar .

Lanarkshire; Scotlands' Middle Earth?

Airdrie's orange, Coatbridge is green
But they all look the same at Hallowe'en

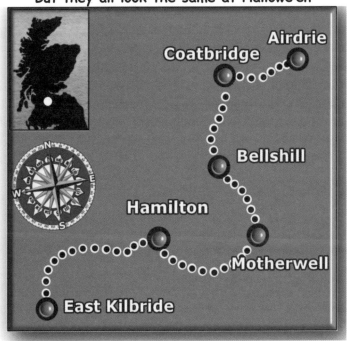

Motherwell-Airdrie-Coatbridge- Bellshill- East Kilbride
(Five Buses-Four 201s' plus a 17)

Lanarkshire; Scotland's Middle Earth?

John; I had been suggesting this trip for ages, not because of it's scenic grandeur, but because the places we would be visiting are real places, with lots of real, and some really crazy people. I'm sure Craig put it off so long because he was feart.

Another reason for this trip is that it is easy to arrange. The old 201 bus leaves East Kilbride and goes to all these places and a few more that even I didn't want to visit.

In the old days this was mining country, so I thought Craig would have something in common with a lot of the older guys as he comes from Auchinleck, which, as you all know, was mining village somewhere in darkest Ayrshire.

The day started with a bit of a shock. After I made my usual Corned Beef with English Mustard on Plain Bread, I kissed the luckiest girl in the world goodbye and headed down to pick up Craig at 10.30am.

He appeared at the door all ready to go but without any sign of his usual pack of pieces with all the extras that Irene usually includes. I asked him where his pieces were, to which he replied, she never made me any.

This was very unusual, and I thought there must have been a wee tiff of some sort, but he assured me that all was ok but that he was none too chuffed.

I sometimes think we give these women of ours too much freedom to make their own minds up and they are starting to take advantage. I feel safe to say this as I am sure Kate's stopped reading the nonsense I write about our trips.

It was a lovely day. The weather this summer and autumn (so far) had been crap, but Craig and I have had good weather on most of our trips. The sun shines on the righteous.

We wandered down to the bus stop and got our bus passes out so there was no rush when the bus arrived. Craig keeps worrying I'll give the driver my credit card again. The old 201 arrived on time. No idea what on time was as there's one every 10 minutes or so at that time in the morning.

Lanarkshire; Scotland's Middle Earth?

Our original plan (and this was Craig's idea) was to get the bus to the furthest point, which was Airdrie, and stop off at the other places on the way back. This was a great idea as if we did it the other way, the last bus journey would be a very long one with the bladders in 15 minute release mode.

I had printed out the timetable on my new laser printer, which is magic, and black only, which is magic as well. On reading it I noticed that the time from EK to Airdrie, the furthest town, was about an hour and forty minutes. This is a long journey on a bumpy 201 even without a bevy. The other problem is that Craig's back is playing up, so as we passed through Hamilton we decided that we would get off at Motherwell first for a pint then go from there to Airdrie, so breaking the journey out into two manageable 50 minute journeys. So this is what we did.

Craig; They say it is useless to try to put off the inevitable. They're right. For as long as we have been travelling around on the old bus pass John has been trying to persuade me to join him on a trip to the dark side: Airdrie and Coatbridge. Up until now I have always managed to come up with a plausible excuse for heading in the exact opposite direction. Unfortunately John is very persistent. He wore me down, caught me off guard or maybe he just got to me when I was slightly under the influence. Whatever the reason for it the fact is that one sunny Friday morning I found myself sitting on the First Bus number 201 to Airdrie.

I'm no stranger to the 201 but I've never been any further than Hamilton on it. It's a fairly bog standard single decker bus which is fine for short journeys. They are just a wee bit basic in the shock absorber department. Not to mention an almost total lack of padded upholstery. Unfortunately my back was giving me gyp that day and the thought of sitting in that bone shaker for an hour and a half was more than I could take.

We reckoned that if we split our journey up, not only would my poor old back be spared a great deal of pain, but we would get our feet on the sawdust three quarters of an hour ahead of schedule.

John; When we got off the bus, Craig suggested we wander down the street and find a Gregg's so he could get a sausage roll. I had a feeling that he had got no breakfast from Irene either. I'll have to weedle the truth out of him after he's had a few pints.

We wandered down a shopping arcade, and the first sausage roll place we found was an Aulds'. Craig went in and got one. He said it was delicious, he must have been starving.

Here's a turn up for the books, we actually start our day off with a visit to the Horseshoe Bar.

These shopping arcades in all towns in Scotland are getting more and more depressing. More of the stores are closed and the majority of the people are looking poorer and poorer. It's maybe only me, but I think this recession is getting worse and is not finished by a long way. I wish Craig had never wanted a sausage roll. If I could go from buses straight into pubs and kid on the real world didn't exist, I would be a lot happier. But there you are!

The pub we visited in Motherwell was '*The Horseshoe*'. Same name as my favourite pub in Glasgow. Although it was only about 11.30am, there were a few people in the pub. The place was spotless, without smelling of bleach, and the bar was roughly the shape of a Horseshoe.

The beer was ok and the bar was nice, but the people in it kept to themselves, as did the barmaid. But it was a good pub and we enjoyed our first pint of the day.

Barmaid Rating; 🍺🍺.

We wandered out and started to wander up to the bus stop when a 201 appeared. Craig cannot move very quickly, not just when its his round, so I ran on ahead to hold the bus. Craig eventually got on and the bus sat for another five minutes. It's always the same, if we had walked, the driver would have buggered off just to annoy us.

We knew that the bus would pass through Bellshill and Coatbridge, as well as other wee places like Whinehill, before arriving at Airdrie, so we kept an eye open for pubs to visit on the way back.

We had never been this way before, and some of the places looked a bit rough, but the people looked great, or just like us, so we reckoned the pubs would be great.

Before reaching Airdrie, the bus detoured into Monklands Hospital where Mary, my daughter-in-law works taking X-rays. It looked a right busy place.

The 201 took us into the main street in Airdrie and the sun was trying to shine as we got off the bus. The main street was busy and the people looked brighter and happier than the sausage roll eating lot in Motherwell. We walked up and down the street for a couple of minutes and clocked about five pubs that could be visited. We settled on '*The Mason's Arms*' for our first port of call. I don't know why as neither Craig nor I are in the Masons. I never joined the Masons for one very important reason, nobody asked me!

Craig; *Motherwell is about the half-way point between East Kilbride and Airdrie so that is where we hopped off the bus. Before finding a pub I suggested we take a short stroll around the town centre. My motive was not, as you may think, to get a little exercise, but to find somewhere to buy some pastry covered meat. I was starving. Due to a slight misunderstanding Irene had forgotten to make me up any sandwiches. This amused John no end and he kept going on about it all day. After a very tasty sausage roll we set about the serious business of the day, finding a decent boozer.*

The Horseshoe Bar seemed like a good prospect to start off our day. It was a good old fashioned man's pub, so it was ideal for us then. I like these old, solid no frills type of pubs. The bar had high ceilings and plenty of floor space, with seating around the walls. It did have the now obligatory flat screen telly on the wall, but nothing over the top.

We didn't manage to talk to anyone as the regulars were keeping very much to themselves. All except one strange wee bloke who was having an animated conversation with himself. We didn't like to interrupt just in case he was making an important point.

Back on board the uncomfortable 201 we made our way towards Airdrie. That's when things got a little strange as far as I'm concerned. Actually it was Coatbridge which caused all the confusion. I was convinced that we had arrived in Airdrie a bit ahead of schedule. This kind of thing happens all the time to us, so I had no suspicion that anything was wrong. John often arrives at our destination thinking we have lost an hour or so. In his case this is usually down to an over indulgence in alcohol. With me it's just a very shaky grasp of geography.

Lanarkshire; Scotland's Middle Earth?

The thing is, when I spotted the large, imposing 'Savings Bank of Airdrie', I assumed that we were actually in Airdrie. But no, we were in Coatbridge. It seemed to me that someone had gone to a great deal of trouble to create a very expensive and not very funny practical joke.

I don't suppose either Airdrie or Coatbridge see a great many tourists. They've certainly never been mentioned in any of the 'Rough Guides' I've ever read. However, it must be a bit of an annoyance to the few poor souls who do travel through this area to find that they are miles away from where they thought they were.

I'm convinced that it would be quicker to walk from Motherwell to Airdrie than take this bus. We must have seen every housing scheme in the area. Thanks to all of this birling about I had no real idea where we were when we actually got there.

John; It was a very busy pub for that time of the day and everybody was talking to each other and enjoying themselves. We were included in the banter by the men at the bar and we had a really great time there. The barmaid, called Carol was really great and was wearing a very smart top with The Masons Arms on her chest, no idea where his hands were.

We got round to telling her and anybody who would listen about us doing our travels and I think they were a bit unsure if we were on the level. However, I had a couple of copies of our first book with us and when she had a look through it, was so impressed that she bought one. So did the man standing next to us. He gave me a tenner and told me to put the two pounds change into the jar on the bar where they save up money for the main charity supported by 'The Mason's Arms', which I think is called 'Help for Heroes'.

It is a great cause to help raise money to support wounded British Soldiers. The specific regiment they supported was the 36th Ulster Division, nothing like nailing your colours to the

227

mast. They were also selling wrist bands for two pounds each for the cause, and since everybody had been so nice and had bought two books, I felt I should buy a wristband, and was happy to do so. I wore it with pride.

We had a couple of pints and would have liked to stay longer as it was a great pub, one of the best we have ever visited. However, as you know, we are not out for the day to enjoy ourselves, but to give feedback on the various pubs and people we meet on our travels. So with sad goodbyes and ten minute handshakes we left the pub, but promised to return, which we definitely will do if we are ever in the Airdrie area.

Barman Ratings; RRRR.

Carol surprised us by buying one of our books.
Personally I think she did it just to stop John talking.

Lanarkshire; Scotland's Middle Earth?

Craig; *Airdrie looked pretty much as I had expected it to look, exactly like any other town in Lanarkshire. I would have to admit that I had no great expectation of finding a really good pub in the place. It was just by sheer chance that we decided to visit 'The Mason's Arms'. Some might call it abject laziness that we decided to visit the pub nearest the bus stop we had just got off at, but I prefer to think of it as fate.*

Before we entered the pub we agreed to stay away from all the usual Masonic jokes and just concentrate our efforts on enjoying a couple of beers. I had good reason to be cautious about this as I've been in this position before.

Many years ago as one of a group of social drinkers I was invited to take part in a general knowledge quiz at the town's masonic lodge. It quickly descended into chaos. Some of my team mates couldn't resist the opportunity to poke fun at our masonic opponents. They didn't appreciate our humour. Halfway through the game our hosts declared themselves the winners and presented themselves with a trophy. We were never asked back.

Although The Masonic was only our second pub of the day we saw that a definite theme was developing. Hallowe'en seems to be very popular nowadays, and neither of us could understand why. I have always thought that Hallowe'en was generally meant to be a time for kids to enjoy themselves. It now seems to be an adult festival, if the decorations in all of these pubs are anything to go by. Personally, I am of the opinion that if a grown man dresses up in a scary costume to wander about the town after dark then he is in all likelihood a stalker, or worse, and should be treated accordingly.

The pub was in the process of being tarted up to look like some sort of grotto, but, thankfully, it wasn't really over the top. Obviously that didn't stop us having a wee rant about it all though.

Lanarkshire; Scotland's Middle Earth?

The bar was quite busy and everybody seemed to be enjoying themselves. We got into conversation with the barmaid, Carol, and she told us all about the big party they were having in the pub that night. I think it was John who suggested that we could come disguised as authors. This let him launch into his sales routine. We had brought a couple of copies of our last book along just in case we met a few likely customers. I really didn't think we had much of a chance of flogging them in this pub.

Carol didn't seem like the type who would buy our book, being the wrong gender and at least 30 years too young to appreciate codger humour. In fact I don't think she even believed we had written a book at all. I suppose that in her line of work she must have heard every unlikely tale ever told.

To his credit John persevered and explained what the book was all about. What finally convinced her was actually seeing the book which was lying on the bar. We had forgotten to show her it, we really are pretty poor salesmen. I think she bought it for her dad.

A few minutes later, one of the customers at the bar decided to buy the remaining book. What a pub!

I've unfortunately forgotten the guy's name but he was good to talk to. He gave us the low down on the other pubs in Airdrie and a couple he knew in Coatbridge.

We had managed to knock back a couple of pints by this time and knew it was time to move on, but we were sorely tempted to stay on for a while. Even as we said our goodbyes our new best pal offered us another drink. It takes great strength of character to turn your back on such generosity, but that's the kind of stuff we're made of.

John; We wandered out and had another look about on the high street before deciding to visit '*The Imperial*'. We knew that after '*The Mason's Arms*', we would be hard pressed to find a pub as good, and we were right. '*The Imperial*' was a good pub, busy and had a good atmosphere. Again, the people looked fairly prosperous and were all enjoying themselves. We felt that although there was nothing at all wrong with the bar, we didn't enjoy it as much as *'The Mason's Arms'*. We enjoyed our pint however, and our overall impression of the part of Airdrie we visited was that it is a great wee place. The bar was very busy and we had no opportunity to try and talk to the barman, so it is hard to give a rating, so I won't.

A funny thing about the first three pubs we visited was that although they were all what we would call old men's pubs, they were all decorated for Hallowe'en and were going to be holding parties. I don't think this happened in the past, although it may be a Lanarkshire thing, or possibly in today's recession pubs are trying everything they can to get people into their bars, and good luck to them. All the bars we had been in so far were great and deserve all the custom they can get.

After eating a couple of my pieces in the sunshine at the bus stop, we jumped onto a number 17, I think. This was not the plan, which was to get the 201 all day, but after three pints I was feeling like living on the edge so we took a chance and got the 17.

It was a great wee bus and surprisingly for Scotland, the driver was a great laugh. He kept talking to people and kids sitting at the back of the bus and taking no interest on the road ahead. We assumed he knew the road and sat back and enjoyed the ten minute run along the road to Coatbridge. As we got off the bus everybody was treated like his friend. It was great.

Craig; *We made our way a few hundred yards, not metres, down the road to 'The Imperial' where we hoped to find a pub as good as the 'Masons', but knowing that would be unlikely.*

The Imperial was a lot more modern than I would have guessed from looking at the outside of the building. In fact it looked a bit like a wine bar. That is usually enough to put me right off, but not this time.

Although the bar was quite busy one of the staff spotted us straight away and said he would be with us in a minute.

That's a professional approach to customer service and it's one that is sadly lacking in most people working in the bar trade today. After years of selfless observation, we have noticed that the usual attitude adopted by these people tends to fall into one of three serving strategies. These are, in no particular order:

a) Serve their pals first.

b) Serve the person directly in front of them first.

c) Develop tunnel vision and serve nobody at all until threatened with physical violence.

We didn't manage to talk to any of the customers, in fact we didn't even manage to get a seat. But the beer was more than acceptable and, since that is the most important part of our day out we thoroughly enjoyed our visit to The Imperial.

When we were planning this trip the main 'selling' point of it was the fact that we would only ever need to look out for one bus service, the 201. It's a frequent service, allegedly, with never more than ten minutes to wait for our next bus. I was therefore just a wee bit surprised to see John leap aboard a small shuttle bus which had stopped beside us in the street. It was a bit early on in the day for the alcohol to be clouding his mind so I assumed that he must know what he was doing. Just for a second or two I toyed with the idea of letting him go on alone, while I legged it back to the Mason's Arms for that drink I had been offered earlier. My conscience got the better of me however and I got on the wee bus with him. It wouldn't be fair on the residents of Coatbridge to let him roam around without his carer.

John; Although the bus run to Coatbridge was great, our first impression when we walked up the High Street was that it did not seem as busy a place as Airdrie. Everything seemed a bit run down, although this may just be the streets we visited. The people seemed a bit less affluent and not as bright and cheerful. We smiled as we walked up the high street to try and cheer people up.

We eventually found a pub called '*The Argyll*', which was next door to the 'Knights of Columba', I think. I didn't know anything about the religious leanings of this area, but was beginning to realise that Airdrie and Coatbridge are, in the main, of different religious persuasions. Not that it mattered to Craig and I. Craig's religion is Tennent's Lager.

We wandered into '*The Argyll*' and ordered our pints. It was a very quiet and depressing place, although it also had the Hallowe'en decorations up. Found this funny for Coatbridge as it meant the pub was covered in orange. Business is business I suppose. The barman stood in the corner of the bar studying form with a regular and didn't give us the time of day.

Just as Craig went to the toilet, a wee man came in and stood beside me at the bar. He seemed friendly and asked me where I came from. After we had told each other who we were, I asked him if Coatbridge was all as run down as the street outside. He said it was because of the big supermarkets built on the edge of town and told me a great story about a pal of his who used to own one of those wee corner shops that sold everything, but had to close because of the supermarkets. Anyway, this wee guy called Alex, who owned the shop was visited one day by a salesman who offered him a special deal. 'Buy 10 boxes of this special toothpaste and I will give you five boxes free'.

So Alex says to the guy, 'What do you see on these three shelves over there?' 'Toilet rolls' says the salesman. Alex takes him into the storeroom and asked him 'What do you see on all these shelves'. Toilet rolls' says the salesman.

'If I can't get the bastards to wipe their arses, how can I get them to brush their teeth?'

Craig returned and wondered why I was rolling about laughing. The wee man went away to talk to the barman and we drank our pint and wandered down the street to the bus stop to await the 201 to take us to Bellshill. **Barman Rating;** .

The Argyll Bar. Fifteen minutes we'll never get back.

We got off the 201 at what looked like the main cross in Bellshill and had a wander up and down the streets which seemed a bit busier than Coatbridge.

Craig found a carry-out place and had a wrap with cheese and bacon. He said he had never had anything like it before, it was great. He needed some sustance because he had no pieces.

After wandering about till Craig finished his wrap and after looking at a few pubs we decided on *'The Crown Bar'*

'The Crown' was a nice bar and well set up, including the obligatory Halowe'en decorations. The atmosphere in the place was good and we enjoyed our pint. I wished we had brought more books as I'm was sure we could have sold them to the locals who looked as if they were lusting after knowledge. Although to be fair, one or two of them looked as if they had never been out of Bellshill. The barman was friendly and was very helpful in answering our questions about the religious differences between the three towns we had visited.

Barman Rating; .

Craig; I didn't think it would be possible to find a more uncomfortable bus than the 201 but somehow John had managed to discover one. This metal box on wheels was a nightmare to travel on. The level of comfort it offered would not be acceptable in a third world country. Then again, neither would the road it was forced to travel along.

To take our minds off the shoddiness of both his bus and the lunar landscape we were trundling along, the driver treated us to a comedy routine. Unlike almost every other bus driver we've come across on our travels this guy really had a good sense of humour. He must be new to the job. Give him a couple of years carting the likes of us around the place and he will become as dour and sullen as the rest of them.

As soon as our feet hit the pavement in Coatbridge we headed for the nearest pub. We had long since decided that, given there was absolutely no hint of scenic grandeur to be had on this trip, we would concentrate all our efforts on the appreciation of draught beer.

That's why we ended up strolling into the Argyll Bar. The place was almost empty, and we really should have left it that way. The barman barely acknowledged our existence, which is of course nothing new to us. This was yet another pub which was all done up for a Hallowe'en party. At least I hope it was for Hallowe'en. We drank our beer in almost complete silence, then left without exchanging a word with the barman. In his defence, reading the Racing Times does take a lot of concentration.

Coatbridge probably has many great pubs but, we just couldn't be bothered looking for any of them. Besides, Bellshill was calling.

Once again I have to point out that our little expeditions are more hit and miss than scientific. When we don't actually know much about the town we are visiting, we just get off the bus in the first built up area we come to and hope that we've made it to the town centre. Sometimes we get it right, actually sometimes we never find out whether we got it right or wrong.

Bellshill looked a bit brighter than our last stop, so we thought we were onto a winner. Actually the pub we chose to visit, The Crown, reminded me of a bookies shop. It was bright, noisy and just a bit disappointing. The beer was OK but the atmosphere let it down. There were far too many big flat screen tellies. The fact that they were all showing sport didn't help.

John; Back at the bus stop there was no sign of a bus, but there was a great smell of grease, or creash, if you come from Auchinleck. So I dived in and got a bag of chips which we shared. They were burning hot. It was sad watching Craig having to survive on carry-out food because of the failings of Irene, but he still insisted there was no trouble at mill. We managed to finish them and a bar of chocolate before the 201 arrived.

While we were at the stop there were three wee boys about 12 years old at the most, and what a cheeky shower of wee bastards they were. Just before the bus arrived they stood in front of us and started to give us kids' version of abuse. It was just as well the bus arrived as Craig was about to banjo one of them. They got on the bus as well. There were no parents with them. They probably really were a shower of wee bastards.

This journey to EK would be about 45 minutes so we decided that if either of us was desperate for the toilet, we would get off in Hamilton and have a pint and pee in one of the great pubs there.

As Hamilton came into view our bladders were holding on fine so we decided to hang on till East Kilbride and have a couple of pints in '*The Crooked Lum*', which is the pub just down the hill from our houses.

The journey to East Kilbride passed very quickly as we both slept most of the way. It's funny that when you get old you start falling asleep all the time. Sometimes it can be quite embarrassing.

So we got off the bus and into '*The Crooked Lum*'. While we were in the Lum talking I said to Craig that we should take a photo of the Crooked Lum.

The Crooked Lum is a Crooked Lum which takes the smoke away from the fireplace in the middle of the bar, and it is crooked, hence the name. Craig thought it was a good idea, but thought he should take the photo when the light was better. As you know, Craig fancies himself as a photographer. Ever since his photo of Arran was picked as the cover, and for January, on the Millport Calendar, he thinks he is Lord Snowdon.

I text'd Kate to let her know that I would be home about 7.30pm. She was very surprised. Craig is the ultimate party animal and is seldom home before midnight, if he can help it.

I think he wanted to be home early to see if Irene would have any dinner for him. After all the carry-out food he had eaten, he was craving for mince and tatties. I wonder if it was the cold shoulder he got.

We wandered up the road to our homes. Kate was surprised and happy to see that I was reasonably sober. She worries about me-though God knows why. I've been like this for 64 years.

Craig; Round at the bus stop John couldn't resist buying a bag of chips. I couldn't resist helping him eat them. We had just finished them when we had a run in with the 'Bash Street Kids'. These three cherubic gangsters began jumping around us, shouting, making rude gestures and generally getting right up my nose. No doubt these apprentice neds will one day find their niche in society, probably drinking Buckfast and mugging pensioners.

John suggested that a sustained course of energetic smacking might work wonders for these little treasures. I felt it was my duty to point out that it is socially unacceptable nowadays to smack children. Although, personally I think we should be allowed to tazer the wee buggers.

We decided to make the Crooked Lum in East Kilbride our last stop of the day. Since the bus stopped right outside it, this made perfect sense to me. Over our last couple of brews we reviewed our day's adventure. I have to admit that it had turned out better than I had thought it would. Most of my knowledge of the towns we were to visit was of the hearsay variety, and what was said wasn't good. To be honest, when the person who suggested the journey in the first place described it as 'a trip into darkest Lanarkshire' you don't really start out with high hopes.

Like most of our little trips we had enjoyed a couple of really good pubs, put up with a mediocre one and suffered one that is best forgotten.

Of course we only get to see these places for a short time on a week day afternoon, so we don't always get to see them at their best. I feel I have to say that just on the off chance I ever have to go back there.

In Summary

This was one of our most straight forward trips. We only had to use a single bus route. Simply put, some bits worked better than we thought they would while others did the exact opposite. Airdrie was the star turn of this journey. The pubs were great. That was just as well really as things went rapidly downhill from there on. Happily we understand that there is little chance of this having any adverse effect on tourism in this area of Lanarkshire.

Bar rating 3.2 taking this trip into a surprise 4th place.

A Capital Day Oot

(A great day oot in our capital city
The booze wis great, the price, a pity.)

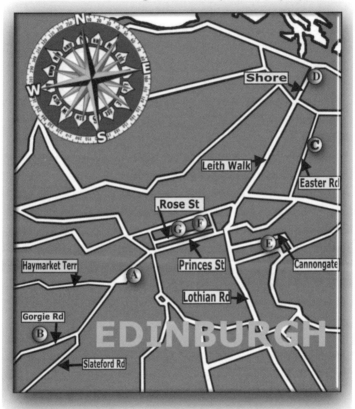

A:- Haymarket Bar,   B:- Tynecastle Bar,
C:- Four in Hand,   D:- Malt and Hops,
E:- The World's End,   F:- The Abbotsford Bar,
G:- Thirty Seven Bar.

*East Kilbride-Glasgow-Edinburgh
Glasgow-East Kilbride*

A Capital Day Oot

John; Craig and I both come from the West of Scotland, Craig from Auchinleck, me from Glasgow, so we don't like Edinburgh or anything associated with it. The people are stuck up, tight fisted and miserable, or so the people of Glasgow are supposed to think.

But to travellers like Craig and me, the truth is very different. Edinburgh is physically very different from Glasgow, but has many things in common, one being that neither city has trams!

But on a serious note, who am I kidding, on to our trip to Scotland's Capital.

Our plan was that we would go to pubs, not just in the centre of Edinburgh, but we would visit the less touristy bits where we would be more likely to meet normal Edinburgh people.

A reasonably early start was needed, I picked Craig up at 9.15am. This is reasonably early for oldies like us.

It was a miserable day, but the forecast for Edinburgh was that it should be dry in the afternoon. Nobody mentioned about the freezing temperatures we would have to endure for our art.

We got our usual Bus No. 18 at the foot of Craig's street and all went well until we turned up towards Union Street, just outside 'McSorlies Bar' and the Bus broke down. The engine was still revving but it could not get into gear. A bit like Craig some mornings!

Luckily for us, this was about the first time that it did not matter when we arrived at the bus station as there is a bus to Edinburgh every 15 minutes.

Craig wanted to wait for the next No. 18, but I realized that if we walked through the Heilandmans' Umbrella and into Hope Street we would get a choice of dozens of buses to take us up to the bus station.

As soon as we arrived at the bus stop a No. 9 stopped, picked us up and took us up to the bus station, Craig was suitably impressed, even if he didn't say so.

A Capital Day Oot

Craig; *Having visited three of the main towns on the east coast it was decided, not by me, that we just had to complete the set by spending the day in our capital city. Against my better judgement it was finally agreed that we should visit my least favourite of all Scottish towns, just after Christmas. Even before we started out it looked like things were unlikely to work out too well.*

John has the very annoying habit of always being on time. Not just on time but exactly on time. That might not sound like much of a cause for complaint but, it must be remembered; I'm easily annoyed first thing in the morning. The thing is no one can be as exact as he is, not without cheating anyway. It's just not possible to arrive at the precise time, every time.

My personal theory is that he hides behind the hedge at the top of my street and waits there until it's time to appear at my front door. It annoys me so much that I've taken to standing behind the door, ready to whip it open just before he can knock on it. Sometimes it's hard to tell which of us is the weirder.

Anyway, on the appointed day I was, as usual, lurking behind the door waiting to pounce when something strange happened, or rather didn't happen. John was a no-show. Five minutes doesn't sound like much of a delay but, when you're hiding behind your own front door, it seems like an age.

It turns out that John had left his house bang on time to take up his usual position behind the hedge but had to turn back. He'd forgotten his bus pass. There was a certain amount of irony in there, given that you get one because of your age, and then you forget it for the same reason.

Anyway we missed the bus by a couple of minutes. It shot past us as we walked along the road towards the bus stop. Like a true professional I didn't utter a word of criticism. I confined myself to a lot of meaningful staring.

The actual journey down to Glasgow was fairly standard. As usual the bus had to follow a detour down Strathclyde Street in the Dalmarnock area of the city. This is where a lot of travelling people have their caravans. We have been along this road so often in the last few months that I half expected the folk down there to wave to us as we passed through.

The first time we encountered this diversion it caused us quite a bit of worry. We thought that it would make us late for our connecting bus. As it turned out it didn't then, or any time since. Nowadays we had no worries about keeping to our timetable, or so we thought.

It wasn't the bus breaking down which annoyed me, it was the fact that the driver didn't seem to know it had broken down. He just sat there revving the engine for about ten minutes before he gave up and told us all to get off.

John, still feeling guilty about his part in missing the bus earlier, was desperate to find us another lift to the bus station.

To cut a long story short, and to listen to John's explanation, it would be a very long story indeed, we arrived at Buchanan Bus Station in time for our bus to Edinburgh.

Considering this trip was all John's idea I was amazed to find out that his entire master plan for the day consisted of catching the 'Intercity' bus and then 'winging it'.

John; There was an Edinburgh bus waiting, the Number 900, and the majority of oldies must have been having a long lie or sheltering from the weather because there was hardly anyone waiting.

We got our pick of the seats and settled down for our trip to the Capital. It was a nice journey. The M8 and the surrounding area look much better from a coach seat than it does if you are driving a car.

After passing the Airport you come across a huge, newly built tram terminus with no trams, or tracks. It is very strange. In fact the whole Edinburgh Tram scheme is crazy. The first thing that seems crazy is that it is planned to start about a mile or so from the Airport. Why did they not plan to take the trams right into the Airport. There doesn't seem to be any physical obstacle to doing this. They will have their reasons I'm sure.

My other thought is why have trams in the first place. If the idea is to have people transported quickly through Edinburgh in the middle of the road, why not just have a bus only bit in the middle of the road. If they're so keen to use electricity they could strap a few wires between lamp posts and have Trolley Buses, or the silent death as we used to call them in Glasgow.

Nothing seems to make sense to me. At this stage Craig was completely brassed off listening to me going on about it, so I shut up, But just for a minute.

We got off the bus at Haymarket. Craig's plan was to get a bus from there to the Tynecastle area and our first pub. The problem was that it was pouring, so we dived across the road and into 'The Haymarket Bar'.

Decision time in the Haymarket.

It was a nice, up-market type of bar. It was right into the real ales. There must have been about 20 pumps in a row along the bar. I asked for a pint of lager for Craig and a pint of heavy or 70 shilling for myself. You would have thought I'd asked for a piece of the moon. The guy said to pick from the thousand pumps in front of me. I chose a pint of Excelsior, I think it was called. It was not too strong. Some of these real ales will knock your head off. It was actually very nice and I could have gone a few of them, but the rain was off and the sun was shining, so we finished our pints and headed out to get our bus. It was absolutely freezing. Although Edinburgh gets less rain that the West, when it's cold it's freezing.

Barman rating; 🅡🅡🅡.

Craig; Fortunately, as usual, I had spent hours on my computer planning the best route around town. Actually I had an ulterior motive. Auchinleck Talbot, my local junior football team, was going to play Hearts in the fourth round of the Scottish Cup the following week and I had a ticket. Needless to say I had earmarked Tynecastle as an area of interest for our day out.

We got off our Citylink bus at Haymarket with the intention of catching a local bus down Gorgie Road to a pub I had checked out on the internet. Unfortunately between us and the bus stop sat The Haymarket Bar and John was ready for beer. I'm really glad he was for two very good reasons. It turned out that the Haymarket Bar was a really great pub and I really needed a beer as well.

The bar was very bright, tidy and well laid out. In fact it seemed a wee bit too up-market to be calling itself a bar, but that's Edinburgh for you.

As soon as I saw the set-up on the bar I knew we were in trouble. There were far too many beer pumps. John would never be able to choose which one to try. He usually opts for a pint of Best which has all the alcoholic properties of oxtail soup, but all of these beers were a bit on the strong side.

A Capital Day Oot

The barmaid was very helpful, not to mention patient, and suggested a couple of beers John might like. I suggested that she should just half fill a glass with any of them then shove in a handful of ice cubes to water it down.

The owner, and or manager, came over to give us the benefit of his expertise. He reeled of the name of every beer, where they were brewed and their different strengths. In other words he made a difficult choice impossible. In the end John just pointed at the pump nearest to him and asked for a pint.

My pint of very ordinary lager was very good and John claims that his pint of whatever was not too bad either. The price was a bit of a shocker though. Maybe we were paying tourist rates.

John; There were three bus stops together at which different numbered buses stopped, but there was a clear set of instructions to tell you which one to stand at, so we knew which one was ours. Our bus came round the corner, went by our stop and stopped at the next one. To be honest, we were not surprised. We are crap at reading this sort of stuff. You'd think we would get better with all the travelling we do, but we don't. The bus driver was very nice and waited for us. No way would he get a job in Glasgow.

I put my card down and said we were going to Tynecastle. He replied that he didn't' care where we were going as it was all the same cost-nothing. You don't get a ticket either. This is different from Glasgow. But it's all free so we didn't care.

Craig had been on Google as usual, using his new magic phone and knew where we were going. Sure enough we were only on the bus (Number 25) for a few minutes when we spotted the floodlights of Tynecastle, where Hearts play, so we got off and wandered about till we spotted a pub called *'The Tynecastle Bar'*. Goodness knows how they thought that one up.

It looked the sort of pub we like, a dump, so in we went. It was great inside with photos of Hearts players and other memorabilia covering the walls.

The barman came over right away and asked what we wanted. While he was pouring the pints he said that we were pretty old and should know the answer to a question the co-owner of the bar wanted desperately to know, what was the name of the wee barmaid in 'Cheers'. Although we took offence at the old reference, Craig couldn't help himself and shouted out Carla.

How pathetic is that? Craig watches a lot of telly and has a great memory.

We enjoyed our pints and told the barman about what we were doing and showed him our first book. That was the last we saw of him. Are Edinburgh people really tight fisted or were we just boring the poor guy to death; probably the latter.

Barman rating; .

Edinburgh in December, Very bracing!

Craig; After a wee misunderstanding at the bus stop we caught the No 25 down to Tynecastle. Using the magic of the internet I had already checked that there was a suitable watering hole close to our bus stop.

A Capital Day Oot

The Tynecastle Bar, as you might expect, was painted in the colours of Hearts football club. Inside it was the same story, maroon everywhere. I did notice that in pride of place behind the bar was a large plaque commemorating some great win over their arch rivals Hibs. This apparently took place in the mid 1990's, which wasn't exactly yesterday, but is still very important to the people on this side of the city.

We bought a couple of reasonably priced, ordinary, pints from a chatty young barman. Actually he was chatty right up to the point where there was an outside chance that money might be crossing the bar in what for him would be the wrong direction. John had produced the book from my rucksack.

The young guy all but sprinted to the far end of the bar, and stayed there until we left the premises. That's Edinburgh for you.

Just to keep things balanced we thought it would be a good idea to visit the area where Edinburgh's other football team is located. Even if the city centre hadn't been turned into a massive building site I would have struggled to navigate my way to Easter Road. As it was I had no idea where I was at any time on our journey on the No1. It was only by sheer luck that I caught sight of the name of a side street I remembered from my computer searching.

John; We left the pub, shouting our goodbyes to the missing barman and wandered out to find the nearest bus stop. Craig had checked out that it was the No. 1 bus that would take us to our next port of call, Easter Road.

There was a timetable on the shelter which told us that there was a bus due in five minutes. This gave me enough time to nip along to a Hole in the Wall for some money, I had forgotten to bring some when I left the house this morning. Craig had kept reminding me to get money. Think he was worried he'd have to buy the drinks all day.

247

The bus turned up dead on time and we showed our cards to the driver and were on our way to the Hibernian side of town.

It is fairly obvious from all the buildings you see in Edinburgh that it has never had the same amount of dirty type employment that Glasgow had in the past. All the buildings looked really nice.

The bus took us along a bit of Prince's Street, which I think has the title of the most beautiful street in Europe. I would agree that if you are on Prince's Street and looking over the gardens towards the castle the view is stunning, but, like everywhere else, some of the recent building additions to the street are pretty awful, and with more phone shops and the like, the street itself is not as beautiful as it once was, still nice though.

The bus wandered through nice streets and down Easter Road going towards Leith. We got off again when we spotted the Hibs ground and wandered into a pub called *'Four in Hand'*.

The pub was a bit run down although there was nothing really wrong with it. The walls were covered in Hibs strips and memorabilia.

We were interested in finding out if there was a story behind the name of the pub, but as soon as the barman served us he went away to a corner of the pub and sat down and read his paper. What's that all about, a barman should always welcome strangers and talk to them, if they want him to. Is this too much to ask? That was the last we saw of him so we finished our pints and got the hell out of the bar.

Barman rating; 🍺.

Craig; Once off the bus we very quickly found a likely looking pub on Easter Road. The exterior of the pub itself was, as you might expect, painted in the colours of its famous local football team, Hibernian. It certainly looked like a nice place to pass an hour or so but, unfortunately It cheated its looks. Maybe at another time of day or certainly on a match day the 'Four in Hand' would be a very different pub.

A Capital Day Oot

There were only a couple of other customers in the bar. Actually, it turned out that one of these 'customers' was in fact the barman. He was extremely busy reading a book and didn't seem to appreciate being interrupted by pesky customers. We had decided to find out the story behind the name of the pub but didn't get the chance to bring it up in conversation, mainly because we didn't have a conversation. As soon as he had dumped our pints on the bar he was away back to his book. Maybe he had reached a very exciting part of his book, or, maybe he was just a rubbish barman who knew nothing about customer service.

With nobody to talk to we just sipped our beers and looked around the place. I noticed a plaque on the wall which commemorated a famous victory over Hearts in some very important game in the dim and distant past. It was de'ja vous, all over again.

John; Of all the areas we visited this was the poorest looking, although this is only by Edinburgh standards. The whole place is pretty flash.

Our next bus was the No. 35, which again arrived on time and took us on the short journey down to Leith.

Leith is a really up-marked place with fancy flats, restaurants and waterside bars. We wandered about looking for a bar that fitted into our ethos. (pretty flash use of the language, hope it's in the right context).

We wandered into a bar called *'The King's Wark'*, walked round the small, very fancy bar, and straight out the other door. Everybody in the place was sitting at tables eating different types of seafood. The smell was terrible, I hate seafood.

Eventually, two minutes later, we found a bar called *'Malt and Hops'*. This was a nice wee bar with a real fire which was great because we were freezing. The barmaid was very pleasant and the place sold ordinary lager and beer. It seemed out of place for its surroundings. We couldn't spend too long in each place because of our tight schedule so we only had one pint, but would advise anybody visiting Leith to give it a visit.

Barmaid rating; ▯▯▯▯.

We must have waited about 15 minutes for our next bus, although it seemed like hours as it was so cold. It was the No. 36 which was going all the way to the Parliament Buildings.

By the way, on a trip to Edinburgh with Kate last summer we walked by the Scottish Parliament Building. I know everyone has their own opinion of this building, but I think it is the ugliest building I have ever seen, and why put it right in an area of lovely buildings? It is so out of place. The front looks like one of these Spanish Hotels in the middle of construction. You know with the wooden poles that seem to be holding up the floor above. Anyway, back to our trip.

The reason for getting this particular bus was that Craig wanted to visit a pub called *'The World's End'*. The bus seemed to go around the whole of Edinburgh before we went round a corner and the pub was right in front of us. Even Craig, who had arranged the buses was amazed, although he didn't admit it.

The pub was packed with people who all looked like they were members of The Young Conservatives. Interbreeding was evident all around. Everyone to their own I say and we had no trouble getting our pints. Mind you, I'm not surprised. Two pints cost us £6.94. This was a record for us, one not to be repeated. Finishing our pints we headed for the door. The pub was nice enough, but is set up for the upper classes and tourists. The two people behind the bar were not the type who wanted to talk to us, so we didn't try.

Barmaid Rating; ▯.

Craig; Our next bus arrived bang on time yet again. All this efficiency was beginning to make an impression on us. Up at Leith the bus let us off on a narrow cobbled street next to the Water of Leith. The whole area has been severely redeveloped. Even the cobbles were new. All it needs to make this place

*really special is an efficient tram service. I'm surprised no one
has thought of that.*

*We wandered around for a little while taking photographs but
it was absolutely freezing so we took shelter in a nearby pub.
However that pub, The King's Wark, turned out to be more of a
restaurant than a pub. Without a word being spoken, both of us
instinctively headed for the exit. I had the feeling that we had
just saved ourselves a small fortune as this place looked really
expensive.*

*Just along the road we found a much better prospect. The Malt
and Hops was a wee bit old fashioned, but in a good way. That
is to say it was a real pub, not one of those fake, theme pubs we
both hate. It had a great roaring fire which we much
appreciated as we did the reasonably priced pints.*

*The barmaid was very pleasant and chatted away to us as she
worked. She managed to keep everyone served and tidied the
place up at the same time. We were impressed. Most of the bar
staff we come across can hardly be bothered putting beer into
a glass never mind keeping the bar clean.*

*While we waited for our next bus, and the possible onset of
hypothermia, a thought occurred to me. In all the time we had
been wandering around the place, taking photos and drinking
beer, not once had we caught sight of a single 'Leith
poleithman'. Maybe the cold, or the booze, was getting to me.*

*By the time we got back into the city centre it was dark, which
didn't help my navigational skills. Once again it was down to
sheer luck that we managed to find our next pub, although we
didn't feel too lucky when we went inside. It turned out that all
our efforts to get to the very crowded 'World's End' were a
waste of time. I think we were the oldest people in the place by
a good thirty years. Fortunately I had enough beer in me to be
immune to any age related embarrassment.*

*The one good thing about all these pretty young things being in
the pub was that they were so busy pretending to be witty and*

interesting they weren't drinking very much. That meant we had no problem ordering our beers.

John; We wanted to finish our Edinburgh trip with a visit to Rose Street, so we walked up the Royal Mile for a wee bit, and then crossed the bridge at Waverley Station. The wind at this stage would have cut a new gub in you. We went along Prince's Street with the market stalls, mulled wine and all the fairy lights. It was very nice and Christmassy.

Once in Rose Street, the first pub we tried was *'The Abbotsford Bar'*. It was very busy and more like a bar for ordinary people like ourselves. The barmen were rushed off their feet and did not have time to talk to anyone. But they were good and very efficient.

Barman rating; 🍺🍺🍺🍺.

Back out into the freezing night we didn't hang about and went into *'Thirty Seven Bar'*. I think 37 was the address in Rose Street. It was a cosy and friendly bar, but again full of tourists and not the sort of bar for spending time with the barman. But it was very nice and worth a visit.

Barman rating; 🍺🍺🍺.

As usual, after a few pints, we decided to take the train home although the bus had been great and had a toilet. So we wandered through the market in Prince's Gardens and as Craig was looking for something to eat, we had a look at the places serving food. The prices were ridiculous so Craig had to stay hungry at least till we got back to Glasgow.

When we got to the station, we went over to the automatic ticket dispensers and could not work out how to buy a single ticket, but noticed that a 'cheap day return' was £11.40. Where's the cheap part in that price? We found an official lady who knew how to work the ticket machine. Craig nearly fainted when the single ticket turned out to be £11.30.

A Capital Day Oot

After getting over the shock, we thanked the lady for trying to rip the piss out of us and we both decided to head for the bus, dodgy toilets or not.

Craig; *After a forced march from the Cannongate up to Rose Street we found ourselves drinking a rather good pint in 'The Abbotsford'. It was quite a nice old pub with very traditional decoration. The place was fairly busy but we found a wee space at the bar, we always do. The bar staff were quite busy so we didn't manage to chat to them at all. More importantly, we didn't manage to flog them any of the half dozen of our books which John had been carting around with him all day. It would have been quite easy to stay for another pint in The Abbotsford but we thought that it would be a shame to just visit one pub in the legendary Rose Street.*

Bar 37, just along the road, was also 'no bad'. But like all of the pubs in Rose Street, or at least all of the ones I've ever visited, it was a bit tourist orientated. There's nothing wrong with that but it does make it quite difficult to sook up the local culture.

It might have had something to do with the amount of Tennent's lager I had swallowed but, in all of our wanderings I hadn't caught sight of a single chip shop.

That was a bit of a personal disaster. Haddock and chips is my cuisine of choice after a night of social drinking.

We decided to give the Christmas market on Prince's Street a go in our search for food. The only food on sale that I recognised as edible was a' toastie'. This sounded fine to me until I saw how much they expected me to part with for a couple of grams of waxy cheese and two scraps of singed bread.

Things got no better down at Waverley Station. We had decided to get the train back to Glasgow. At least that was the plan until we found out how much Scotrail intended to extort from us for the privilege. We would have been cheaper getting a taxi. Actually, using one of those budget airlines, we could have flown from Edinburgh to London then back up to Glasgow for roughly the same price as this train journey. We caught the bus instead, for free.

John; We found the bus station without any problem, used the 30p toilet for one pee and got on the bus, which was free. There was definitely a toilet, so we were quite relaxed.

By the time we were on the outskirts of Edinburgh we were both sound asleep and the next thing I knew was Craig was telling me we were in the Bus Station in Glasgow. What a great journey, and I wakened up feeling like a pint. What am I like?

Craig in particular was hungry, and on the corner of West Nile Street and Hope Street there is a Blue Lagoon fish and chip shop, magic.

Craig has been asking me recently if I knew what a Pizza Crunch was. I explained that it was half a pizza deep fried and crunchy. He said he fancied trying one, so when we went into the Blue Lagoon I noticed they made them so we ordered one. I think it had been lying in the glass heating compartment for at least a day because it was soft and soggy. I thought it tasted great, but could only manage a couple of bits. Craig was the same and most if it ended up in a bin. Mind you, the chips were great, lovely and soft.

By the time we finished the chips we were outside the *'Horseshoe Bar'*, so in we went for a couple of pints. Pints and service were great as usual. By this time we were starting to talk a load of rubbish, I think.

We wandered into The Central Station and caught the 10.18pm train. Craig phoned Irene who was waiting for us at East Kilbride Station. What a woman! So ended a great day.

Edinburgh is definitely a place worth a visit. It has lovely buildings and many good pubs, but it is very busy and a lot of tourists are floating about. But overall a great place, not as good as Glasgow, but still great.

A Capital Day Oot

Craig; *John insisted on sitting in the very front seat which meant everyone getting on to the bus had to pass us. Since we both fell asleep straight away I have no idea what horrible sights they must have witnessed. I very much doubt we were looking at our best.*

Back in Glasgow we began the search for a good chip shop. We found 'The Blue Lagoon' instead. John loves this shop and I was too hungry to keep on looking. Just for a change I decided to try a different meal. And different is what I got. For months John had being going on about something called 'Pizza Crunch. I wish I had never heard of the dammed thing. It was disgusting. I managed a bit off each corner before I was forced to bin the rest of it. Even then it was still better than a £4.00 toastie.

To get rid of the taste of the 'crunch' I suggested a trip to the Horse Shoe Bar. John seemed quite keen. A couple of pints later I was feeling much better.

Before we set off on this trip I was quite certain that I wasn't going to enjoy it. I was wrong. We had visited a couple of pubs which, quite honestly, didn't deserve our, or for that matter anyone else's custom. However, the good ones outweighed the bad ones. On top of that the scenery in and around Edinburgh was well worth the effort of travelling there.

I was also impressed with the buses in Edinburgh. On the whole they arrived and departed at more or less the times they were supposed to, which is very unusual in our experience.

The bus drivers themselves were also a bit of a revelation. Maybe that's because we are so used to the growling and scowling of Glasgow bus drivers. But to suddenly find drivers who were willing to answer direct questions and who don't drive away just as you reach the bus stop is quite amazing.

Edinburgh will definitely be on my list of places to revisit in the future.

A Capital Day Oot

In Summary

Looking back on the day's highs and lows, one thing really stands out; Edinburgh is a very expensive place to get off a bus. We expected it to be like that, but it still came as a shock to be asked to hand over vast amounts of cash for some very ordinary beer.

That being said, there were a couple of really good pubs to be found.

As far as food was concerned we were not very impressed. Granted it was the city centre, and it was a 'special market'. But four quid for two slices of bread is just nonsense. We could only wonder what they would charge if someone was rash enough to ask for the outside slice.

We did like the bus service however. The timetable was spot on, in both directions.

Maybe if they ever finish laying the tram tracks the bus journey could be cut by ten minutes or so.

The bar score for Edinburgh was 2.57, which is not too bad at first glance. However that places it in tenth position in our little league of pubs which, given that there were only thirteen in the league, is a pretty dire performance. This town is by far Scotland's biggest tourist attraction after all. We can only hope that by sheer bad luck we managed to pick the very few truly manky pubs in our capital city.